Teaching Techniques
for Sunday School

UNIT V

BY

CLARENCE H. BENSON, LITT. D.

Edited and Revised by

D. K. REISINGER

EVANGELICAL TEACHER TRAINING ASSOCIATION
1825 College Avenue • P. O. Box 327 • Wheaton, Illinois

Other texts in the Preliminary Certificate Series

OLD TESTAMENT SURVEY—Law and History
OLD TESTAMENT SURVEY—Poetry and Prophecy
NEW TESTAMENT SURVEY
UNDERSTANDING CHILDREN AND YOUTH
SUNDAY SCHOOL SUCCESS

Printed in U. S. A.

*Textbook of the Certificate Course
Unit V*

*Copyright 1935 by Clarence H. Benson
© Copyright 1950, 1959, 1963 by Evangelical Teacher
Training Association
Text revised 1963*

Introduction

Good Christian education is the Church effectively communicating the Word of God. Capable leaders who minister through teaching are needed if growth is to be experienced and the program of God advanced.

Capable leadership begins with dedication and vital concern. It includes preparation and understanding. Church leadership preparation is founded upon teacher training, for in a training program are included foundational courses for all church leadership. TEACHING TECHNIQUES is such a course.

Good teaching has been defined as "a person filled with his subject overflowing to others." It is more than this. An informed person must also direct the flow of the overabounding waters of truth so that benefits can be appropriated by those under his teaching. TEACHING TECHNIQUES helps the teacher to carefully channel the truths he presents so that the purposes of God are fulfilled and the needs of students met.

TEACHING TECHNIQUES is a standard text used by thousands of churches in the preparation of leaders and teachers. Questions and projects in the present edition have been completely revised to allow for varying degrees of depth and emphases. The impact, however, of Dr. Benson's original presentation is preserved. A teachers guide has been prepared to assist the one presenting the course in class instruction.

The book is an integral part of the Evangelical Teacher Training Association program of teacher preparation. When courses are taught by E.T.T.A. approved teachers, the student receives credit applicable to the Association's Teachers Certificate. A further explanation of this program of leadership education is found on pages 94 and 95 under the caption *For Your Information*.

PAUL E. LOTH, Ed.D., *President*
Evangelical Teacher Training Association

Foreword

Marion Lawrance, a great Sunday school worker, once said: "The greatest need in the church today is trained teachers who will put their whole mind into their preparation, their whole soul into their presentation, and their whole life into their illustration." One can hardly find a statement of greater brilliance and insight to describe the nature and work of Sunday school teaching. Here is a challenge which should stir the heart of every Sunday school teacher and worker to be at his best in heart, life, and service for the Lord Jesus Christ.

It gives me great pleasure to recommend the Evangelical Teacher Training Association to the readers of this volume. This evangelical Christian group has stood for orthodox Christianity, training of the workers, and high levels of quality in the ranks of those who serve the Lord Jesus Christ.

Teaching Techniques for Sunday School is an indication of ETTA's desire to extend the kingdom of God through consecrated and trained Sunday school teachers and workers. I am sure that each reader will find, as did the writer, that these materials will prove to be a real source of inspiration and information in the grand task of being co-workers and co-laborers in the Lord's vineyard.

HERBERT W. BYRNE, Ed.D.
*Dean of the College
and Associate Professor of Education
Huntington College
Huntington, Indiana*

Table of Contents

Introduction 3
Foreword 4

Chapter

I. THE TEACHER HIMSELF 7
    Christ's Commission — The Teacher's Own Life —
    The Teacher's Knowledge —
    The Teacher's Responsibility —
    Suggested Questions—Additional Exploration

II. AIMS AND OBJECTIVES OF TEACHING 15
    The Teacher's Aims — Attaining Objectives —
    Suggested Questions — Additional Exploration

III. HOW TO TEACH 22
    The Law of the Teacher — The Law of the Pupil —
    The Law of the Language — The Law of the Lesson —
    The Law of the Teaching Process —
    The Law of the Learning Process —
    The Law of Review and Application —
    Suggested Questions — Additional Exploration

IV. INSTRUCTIONAL AIDS 33
    Impressional Teaching Aids —
    Expressional Teaching Aids —
    Suggested Questions —
    Additional Exploration

V. GATHERING LESSON MATERIAL 41
    Sources of Material — Selection of Material —
    Accumulating Material — Suggested Questions —
    Additional Exploration

VI. ORGANIZING THE LESSON 48
    How To Organize Material —
    Steps in Organizing Material —
    Suggested Questions — Additional Exploration

VII. EFFECTIVE ILLUSTRATIONS 54
    Value — Variety — Illustrations that Live —
    Suggested Questions — Additional Exploration

VIII. ASKING QUESTIONS 60
    Why Ask Questions — Preparation of Questions —
    Helpful Suggestions — Suggested Questions —
    Additional Exploration

IX.	TEACHING THE LESSON	66
	Approaching the Lesson Period — Introducing the Lesson — Developing the Lesson — Closing the Lesson — Suggested Questions — Additional Exploration	
X.	GOOD DISCIPLINE	72
	Setting the Pattern — Example of the Teacher — Orderliness of the Pupil — Suggested Questions — Additional Exploration	
XI.	APPLYING THE TRUTH	79
	Application of the Word of God — Application to the Teacher — Application to the Pupil — Suggested Questions — Additional Exploration	
XII.	TESTING THE TEACHING	86
	The Recitation—The Examination — Bible Tests — Behavior Tests—Attitude and Choice — Suggested Questions — Additional Exploration	
	For Your Information	94

CHAPTER ONE

The Teacher Himself

Thousands jammed the stadium for homecoming day. Excitement was high. Half time scores were tied. The "visitors" band was poised for half-time entertainment. Suddenly the stadium floodlights dimmed and blackened. The home team was using this method to humiliate their opponents. What a foolish, frustrated feeling! Completely outfitted, well-prepared, ready to march—"strike up the band"—yet standing helplessly in the dark.

Many Sunday schools and churches are outfitted, equipped, and ready to go, but their leaders and teachers are in the dark concerning what should be done and how to do it. Sunday school personnel must have clearly defined goals and must know precisely how to reach them. Every Christian educator must realize that *the teacher himself* is the key to successful teaching in Sunday school. Methods and programs will fail unless the teachers are men "full of faith and of the Holy Ghost" (Acts 6:5).

CHRIST'S COMMISSION Christ clarifies the goals of Christian teaching, "Go ye therefore, and *teach* (make disciples of) all nations, baptizing them in the name of the Father, and of the Son, and of the Holy Ghost; *teaching* them to observe all things whatsoever I have commanded you . . ." (Matthew 28:19, 20). Christ's commission includes both education and evangelism.

His educational goal "to observe all things" involves more than mere knowing. It goes beyond believing something or memorizing certain truths. It requires more than simply speaking. Christ did more than impart knowledge and secure perfect recitation. He changed the very actions of pupils. Teaching others to observe Christ's commandments is no easy task. Fortunately, no teacher needs to be in the dark concerning *how* to do his job.

Teaching is a rewarding, thrilling experience. It is equally as Biblical as preaching, or any other method of propagating the Gospel. God extends His Church through "the foolishness of preaching." He edifies it through the simplicity of teaching. These God-ordained procedures are both important. Preaching is proclamation; teaching is impartation. Preaching is presentation; teaching is a probing process. Preaching is reminding a man; teaching is helping him to remind himself. "The pastor is across the street, the superintendent is at arm's length, but the teacher is face to face."

Christ was a teacher, the Master-Teacher. He had something to teach. He wanted to teach. He taught with enthusiasm and authority. He possessed the heart of a teacher. And He has inspired Christians of every generation to "teach others also."

THE TEACHER'S OWN LIFE Every Sunday school teacher who wants to be used of God must face up to three important questions: Is my living God-exalting? Is my message Christ-centered? Is my teaching Spirit-empowered? The teacher who can answer "yes" to each of these will contribute positively to the teaching ministry of the church. "For our Gospel came not unto you in word only, but also in power, and in the Holy Ghost, and in much assurance; as ye know what manner of men we were among you for your sake" (I Thessalonians 1:5). In this passage Paul sets forth three important principles: (1) what the teacher *does* is extremely important, that is, his life example; (2) *what* he teaches is vital, that is, the Gospel; and (3) *how* he teaches is strategic, that is, it must be in the Spirit's power.

A. The teacher's example

A teacher's example either contradicts or underscores what he teaches. The teacher's attitude and the unplanned things he says and does make strong impressions on his pupils. This may be called "incidental teaching," but it is exceedingly important.

The teacher may emphasize the importance of God's Word, but if he always teaches from the Sunday school quarterly, he contradicts what he says. He may teach that the offering is an act of worship, but if he hurries through it to get quickly into the lesson, he cancels out his teaching. The teacher may speak about love, but if he is unpleasant to his fellow teachers and officers, or with his family, he cannot teach with any real results.

Every contact either influences you or someone else. You are either marked or you put a mark upon every person you meet. L. Flora Plummer wrote, "Whenever we break through the conventionality which we use for protection, and enter into the inner circle of the heart of a friend, associate, or companion, we become infected with the perfume, or taint, in the atmosphere of his personality."

B. The teacher's Christian experience

Because teaching is a personal relationship and involves the close association of instructor and pupil, the teacher must really know Jesus Christ as Saviour and Lord.

A leading merchant was asked to suggest half a dozen of the world's greatest salesmen. He named Paul, Luther, Wesley, Whitefield, Spurgeon, and Moody. "These men were eminently successful as salesmen," he wrote, "because they had implicit faith in the house they represented, and perfect confidence that its goods were absolutely needed by the trade. This inspired them with a courage and enthusiasm in the presentation of their wares that demanded and secured attention, and the house was kept busy filling orders."

Today's Christian teacher represents the same "house." There is the same need for God's Word. Success, however, depends upon the enthusiasm the teacher has for the task, and his enthusiasm will be in proportion to his own personal faith.

1. Faith in God

There is no doubt that a "Christian teacher" believes in God, but how far does his faith go? Does he possess an active, vital faith in the Lord Jesus Christ? Has he a triumphant, aggressive faith? The teacher must not only have faith—his faith in God must completely possess him.

2. Faith in the Bible

Again and again Jesus said, "It is written." He knew that "holy men of God spake as they were moved by the Holy Ghost" (II Peter 1:21). Effective Bible teachers, preachers, evangelists, and Sunday school teachers derive their convictions through unswerving faith in and loyalty to the written Word of God. They could not have enthusiastic assurance unless they believed that the Bible is the Word of God. God has written to man, "All Scripture is given by inspiration of God," and the marvel and the wonder of that message should stir the heart of every teacher.

3. Faith in the teaching task

Why are you teaching? To please the superintendent? Because you were elected? Because it is your duty? If that is all, you will have little enthusiasm for your task. But if God has called you to teach, you will believe that this God-ordained ministry is supremely important. If God has set you aside for this particular task, He will fulfill His purpose for you. This knowledge provides dynamic motivation and assures blessed success.

C. The teacher's personality

A man who surrenders to God strengthens his own personality. His powers are enriched by surrender to the Lord and Creator of life. Paul's life was made complete and perfect by his surrender to Jesus Christ. From that hour, for him to live was Christ (Philippians 1:21), and everyone who came in contact with him was electrified by his rich Christian personality. Every Sunday school teacher needs this experience of a Christ-enriched personality.

THE TEACHER'S KNOWLEDGE Every teacher should recognize the importance of his position and should seek to be qualified to fill his place. Those who appreciate the teacher's office will also understand the need of preparation.

Professional men spend years in hard study and application. For example, a doctor will not have time to "look it up" when a patient's artery is severed and his life blood is flowing away. The doctor must "know how" or a life will be lost. An unskilled surgeon could cause a child to be crippled for life. Such mistakes would be tragic, but they are not as serious as the blunder of a teacher who gives the wrong counsel regarding spiritual truths.

Sunday school periods are all too brief. Every minute must be turned to the best possible account. Only the trained teacher can utilize these precious moments to the best advantage. For this reason, every teacher needs adequate preparation. This includes consideration and understanding of the following:

A. Christ-centered message—the Bible

No teacher can teach the Bible effectively unless he has a working knowledge of the sixty-six books. To teach intelligently and practically, the instructor should be familiar with the whole.

In his teaching Paul frequently referred to Christ as the example to be followed. He was not satisfied to state principles. He gave down-to-earth examples from the life of Christ to encourage Christian living.

In order to teach love he said, "walk in love, as Christ also hath loved us, and hath given Himself . . ." (Ephesians 5:2). He illustrated unselfishness, "Let every one of us please his neighbor for his good to edification. For even Christ pleased not Himself; but, as it is written, The reproaches of them that reproached thee fell on me" (Romans 15:2, 3). He clarified the meaning of humility, "Let this mind be in you, which was also in Christ Jesus . . ." (Philippians 2:5).

B. Broad knowledge of related subjects

In addition to a knowledge of the Bible, the teacher should be familiar with any related subjects.

1. Geography

Sunday school pupils need to know the geography of Bible lands. New interest is added when they can identify and visualize the mountains, rivers, and towns. But before the pupil can be taught these facts, the teacher must know them.

2. History

Sunday school pupils will be pleased to learn that their teacher is well informed about world historical events and characters that parallel the narratives of the Bible. The skillful teacher is able to whet their appetites and open up whole new realms of information and interest. He shows them how Bible history and geography fit into secular subjects. He helps them to see that "it is history alone, which, without involving us in actual danger, will mature our judgment and prepare us to take right views."[1]

---

[1] Arthur Bestor, *The Restoration of Learning* (New York: Alfred A. Knopf, 1955), p. 133.

Teachers should become familiar with the historical background of the places in Palestine that have been immortalized by the footsteps of the Lord Jesus Christ.

3. Life and customs of Bible times

Life and customs of the ancients differ widely from those of our day. A working knowledge of ancient habits, customs, ceremonies, and attitudes of Bible times will help the teacher to make lessons "come to life." This will enrich the presentation of every lesson.

C. Spirit-empowered teaching

Paul's teaching was successful because the Holy Spirit was his power. "For our gospel came not unto you in Word only, but also in power, and in the Holy Ghost . . ." (I Thessalonians 1:5). Read also Ephesians 1:15, 16 and Colossians 1:9. When he instructed Timothy to "preach the Word," Paul enunciated basic principles.

Today's teacher must teach *the* message of the Word of God faithfully. He is not called to teach *a message* from the Bible, but *the message* of the Bible. Only in this way will he change the lives of others. (II Timothy 4:2.)

D. The pupils

The teacher should know pupils in general—and his own pupils in particular. Only thus will he find an entrance into their lives. "The child mind," says Patterson Dubois, "is a citadel that can be taken neither by stealth nor by storm; but there is a natural way of approach and a gate of easy entry always open to him who knows how to find it."

In seeking to understand his pupils, the teacher must be sensitive to the needs of the class. Some discipline problems may result from the teacher's lack of skill. Other problems, especially extreme restlessness or lack of response, may be caused by faulty home conditions. "No one questions that family life in America is disintegrating."[2] "Instability is spoken of as the chief characteristic of the modern home."[3]

> "Often it is the teacher who can help parents to understand what harm to the child results from too much television, too little outdoor exercise, or too little rest. Correction of these conditions may bring satisfactory interest and attention into the class. More serious home conditions may be corrected by family counseling or conferences to which the church is now giving attention."[4]

Understanding basic family problems will help a teacher to face his task courageously instead of giving up as a failure.

---

[2]Edwin H. Rian, *Christianity and American Education* (San Antonio, Texas: Naylor Co., 1951), p. 115.

[3]T. B. Maston, *Christianity and World Issues* (New York: Macmillan Co., 1957), pp. 80-90.

[4]Findley B. Edge, *Teaching for Results* (Nashville: Broadman Press, 1956).

E. Techniques of teaching

Textbooks and manuals are valuable aids, but they can never supersede the alert teacher. The radio, movie, and TV are effective agencies in imparting information, but they are subordinate to the living teacher. Said a successful minister recently: "Few pastors have been privileged to be assisted by a more consecrated group of teachers than has been my lot. In addition, many of them had taken courses by correspondence and were exceptionally well informed as to the contents of the Bible. But their consecration and their knowledge of the Bible were not sufficient. They still needed the techniques of teaching to enable them to gain and hold the interest of their pupils."

F. Sunday school organization and administration

According to tradition, Mark Hopkins needed only a log to equip his schoolhouse. Most teachers require more adequate physical equipment to enable them to do their best work. But they also need a knowledge of the administration of the Sunday school and its general overall relationship to the total church program. Today's intricate, correlated program will function more effectively if every member of the Sunday school staff is adequately informed. This knowledge (see *Sunday School Success**) is essential not only for general and departmental Sunday school superintendents, but for all teachers, leaders, and workers. The inter-relationship of all workers is of vital importance.

THE TEACHER'S RESPONSIBILITY

The preparation of a Sunday school lesson can be a delight or a drudgery. Systematic preparation procedures will enrich the entire teaching experience. The observance of the three following steps will glorify every minute of the teacher's preparation and teaching.

A. Keep in training for his task

An athlete must exercise regularly. A musician must practice daily. Likewise a teacher will find his class a satisfying pleasure if he is physically fit, mentally alert, and spiritually alive.

1. Physically fit

Christ can be revealed more clearly through vibrant, healthy bodies that exhibit zest and zeal. Christ came "that they might have life and that they might have it more abundantly" (John 10:10). That includes physical fitness and requires a surrender of our bodies (see Romans 12:1, 2) and constant discipline. There must be sufficient sleep, nourishing food, and proper exercise. In today's pressured world, the teacher should maintain balance and care in everything that affects his physical fitness.

---

*Clarence H. Benson, *Sunday School Success* (Wheaton, Ill.: Evangelical Teacher Training Association, 1958).

2. Mentally alert

An alert mind is essential to successful teaching. Today's public school and college students learn how to reason logically. They would be frustrated by any superficial reasoning in Sunday school. The teacher must think intelligently and analyze carefully. He dare not be "behind the times." He must read widely—Christian magazines, current events, newspapers, devotional literature, Christian fiction. The message of the Gospel cannot be presented adequately by a teacher who has developed careless or sluggish reading and study habits.

3. Spiritually alive

It is not enough to study the Bible. There must be a personal application. The teacher's fidelity to his daily devotions will enable him to present instruction forcibly. Teacher, be much in prayer if you would have the power to be quiet and masterful under every circumstance. Constant fellowship with God will guarantee the poise which is so essential to the Sunday school teacher.

B. Have definite times for study

Certain hours should be set aside each week for lesson preparation. This time should be carefully guarded and nothing permitted to interfere. Teaching is so important that its preparation must not be relegated to the spare moments that are left after everything else has received attention. A secluded spot should be sought and no interruptions allowed until the preparation has been completed.

C. Have a definite program of study

Time will be saved and far more accomplished if the Sunday school teacher establishes a definite, clearly outlined pattern for study. Bible study opens up many avenues of interest. The teacher may be tempted to follow inviting bypaths that are not directly associated with the lesson. Only those who are not easily sidetracked will be able to employ their time to good advantage.

Different ages require different presentations of the truth. All pupils cannot be taught in the same manner. To be prepared for these variants, the teacher must have system in his preparation as well as in his presentation of the lesson. And, in addition, an orderly plan of procedure will make it possible to accomplish much more in a given period of time.

Word to the Student

Three types of review emphases are possible through utilizing the question and project sections. The first section contains direct questions for review. The direct questions are content centered and each is answered in the text content. In review, the student will benefit by studying these questions and also by formulating additional similar questions.

Section one should be used by the student in determining the measure of increased knowledge and for fuller appreciation of the lesson content.

The Additional Exploration section includes discussion questions and projects meant as guides for the student in applying the chapter or investigating related or more specific subjects.

These divisions follow the conclusion of each chapter. They will be helpful only to the measure which the student purposefully uses them.

Suggested Questions for Review

1. What important teaching principles can be observed from Christ's commission?
2. What can we learn from Paul regarding basic teaching principles?
3. How does a teacher instruct by his life?
4. What principles of successful salesmanship are also important in Christian witness and teaching?
5. Discuss three aspects of personal faith which lead to successful teaching.
6. Why is training necessary for every church school teacher and leader?
7. Name at least five major areas in which the teacher should have understanding.
8. State three Bible-related subjects with which the teacher should be familiar.
9. What should the teacher do to assure continued effective lesson preparation?
10. In what three ways should he keep in training for his task?

Additional Exploration

1. Write a summarizing paragraph on one of the following:
   a. What is a teacher?
   b. What is the purpose of Sunday school teaching?
   c. Why does a person *want* to be a Sunday school teacher?
2. Think about a Sunday school teacher who impressed you and meant much to you. List the qualities you admired. Endeavor to determine the comparative value of each quality.
3. Take inventory of your own qualifications to teach. Write the particular need which you hope to have met by studying this course.

CHAPTER TWO

Aims and Objectives of Teaching

Why are you teaching? What is the purpose of the Sunday school teacher's weekly routine? Why all these lesson preparations, project plannings, opening assemblies, offerings, records, class teaching sessions? Why? Because the Bible teaches that we should be "warning every man, and teaching every man in all wisdom; that we may present every man perfect in Christ Jesus" (Colossians 1:28).

THE TEACHER'S AIMS Every Sunday School teacher must be motivated and compelled by clear, well-defined aims. What constitutes such primary objectives? The Sunday school teacher's major responsibility is that of transmitting the Word of God so that every pupil may be transformed by God's grace.

A. Lead pupils to receive and confess Jesus Christ

The Christian teacher must recognize and accept his responsibility to lead each pupil to trust in Christ and accept Him as personal Saviour. The teacher should explain the way of salvation as revealed in God's Word. He should pray for each pupil and seek to bring him to a definite acceptance of Christ. Such decisions may come spontaneously as the culmination of careful teaching. The teacher should never use artificial, high-pressure methods, especially in dealing with younger children.

Acceptance of Christ as Saviour is only the first step. The Christian teacher will also seek to lead his pupils into the place of complete surrender and yieldedness to Him.

B. Present the eternal purpose of God

The more abundant Christian life is the theme of the Christian teacher. "Eye hath not seen, nor ear heard, neither hath entered into the heart of man, the things which God hath prepared for them that love him. But God hath revealed them unto us by His Spirit; for the Spirit searcheth all things, yea, the deep things of God" (I Corinthians 2:9, 10). Scripture testifies to the fact that the greatness of God is unsearchable (Psalm 145:3). It is the Christian teacher's privilege to show God's gracious and glorious purpose for His children and explain the far-reaching happiness that is the portion of every child of God.

C. Direct and guide each pupil to fulfill God's will in his life

God has a plan for every Christian. His Word gives directions for knowing His will. The teacher must obey the divine commission, "Feed my lambs" (John 21:15). Young Christians must "grow in grace, and in the knowledge of our Lord and Saviour Jesus Christ." Christian character results from knowing God's Word, obeying His will, and continually acknowledging Jesus Christ as Lord. This requires daily fellowship with God through prayer. The teacher instructs his pupils in these realities of Christian growth.

1. Worship

Worship is the Christian's experience of God's reality and nearness. It is fellowship with Him. It is part of the teacher's work to cultivate the devotional life of his pupils through the class sessions and the services of the church. Instruction should be given in the meaning of reverence, gratitude, love, and faith. It should include songs, stories, and prayers best suited to the age and experience of the pupils.

Such training requires that the Sunday school be given opportunity to worship as a means of expression. The Word of God bears a vital relationship to such instruction and grows out of it. The entire Bible abounds in expressions which provide acceptable forms of devotion.

2. Consistent Christian living

Our pupils' lives reveal the measure of our success or our failure as teachers. This is true. "Regeneration creates the will to do right . . . The definition of the right is one purpose of the educational program of the church."[1] It is the teacher's responsibility to link the truths taught with the daily lives of the pupils to help them to be "doers of the Word, and not hearers only" (James 1:22). Christians who possess the truth as well as profess it will be transformed.

> "The impartation of knowledge does not complete the Christian educational process. . . For education to be effective, it must lead to action . . . Christian education in the deepest sense takes place in a God-conscious atmosphere. If the Holy Spirit is present to inform, to convict, and to inspire—if He has breathed on the teacher and the pupils, there will be a sense of alertness, aliveness, and anticipation that otherwise will be lacking."[2]

Christian character is dependent upon Christian instruction. If Sunday school pupils do not form habits of attention, interest, and politeness, they will inevitably form habits of inattention, heedlessness, and rudeness. Although the Sunday school teacher has the pupil only a short time each week, impressions can be made and habits established that will prove a blessing throughout life.

Service to the Lord is one manifestation of spiritual growth. The alert

---

[1] Maston, *Christianity and World Issues,* pp. 341-342.
[2] *Ibid.,* p. 343.

teacher will suggest opportunities for such activities in the home, school, and church.

Sunday school provides a large number of service opportunities on a church-wide basis. Officers, teachers, and associate teachers are needed for each department. Many Sunday schools today are employing dozens of regular workers, besides a variable number for special tasks. These opportunities are multiplied when a church operates branch Sunday schools or adds Vacation Bible School and Weekday Religious Education to its program.

ATTAINING OBJECTIVES "Plan your work, then work your plan." The establishment and recognition of teaching aims is only half the battle. Aims and objectives must be accomplished. Different procedures may be required to attain the various aims and objectives. All pupils cannot be taught by the same method. A teacher should use every method, procedure, and approach that will effect success in teaching.

A. Storytelling

Telling the story is the favorite method of teaching Kindergarten, Primary, and Junior departments. Large portions of the Bible are narrative and may be readily reproduced in story form. Jesus was the master story teller. His stories are unsurpassed as models of graphic character painting by means of action and spoken word.

What constitutes a good story? Dr. Goodrich C. White says that it must be interesting, dramatic, full of action, and true to life.

1. Interesting

The entire Bible is a thrilling, fascinating story—any part of it can be made interesting narrative. Probably there is no better teaching method by which attention can be gained and held. This is because interest is aroused at the outset.

2. Dramatic

Bible stories possess conflict, plot, suspense—the characteristics that make a dramatic story. In retelling these stories, verbs will abound, but adjectives should be used sparingly. Sentences must be short—language, simple. By look, gesture, and facial expression the teacher portrays truth, gaining immediate admittance through the eye-gate.

3. Full of action

A good story is "action packed." "Full of action" does not mean "full of words." Often action is intensified by the restriction of words. The stories Jesus told are of achievement. He did not take time to describe His characters, but each character was clearly pictured by his deeds. The story of the Good Samaritan demonstrates this principle (see Luke 10:30-37).

4. True to life

The impossible seldom appeals like that which is in the realm of achievement for every boy and girl. A fairy tale may develop the pupil's imagination, but the true story commands larger interest. It is within the realm of realization. It is the element of truth that characterizes Bible stories and makes them superior to all others.

B. Recitation or immediate class participation

Intellectual development requires more than listening. Pupils fed only with stories will not grow mentally. The mental process of listening must give way to more active participation. The pupil must become involved if there is to be assimilation and reproduction. Education is in reality a drawing-out process, and for this reason class participation through recitation can be of real advantage.

Preparation for recitation encourages the pupil to develop his own initiative. It enables him to come to class with some familiarity of the subject. It provides an opportunity for the teacher to test the pupil's acquaintance with the truth and to discover erroneous thinking on his part. The pupil frequently is helped to clarify his own thinking by orally expressing himself in class. In the event a class member appears intellectually lazy, the teacher has opportunity to challenge him to active participation.

No recitation is successful if conducted simply as routine. To insist that the pupil merely recite in the language of the textbook dulls his originality and fails to call forth any activity except that of memory.

There are three major parts to the recitation method: the assignment, the pupil's study, and the actual class participation.

1. The assignment

If assignments are to lead to successful recitation sessions, the following conditions should be remembered.

a. Plan assignments far in advance.
b. Be certain students understand assignments.
c. Assign only worthwhile material of evident value.

2. The pupil's study

Much depends upon motivation by the teacher as to whether home assignments are boring or adventuresome. Arousing interest and causing the student to see the benefits of accomplishment are key factors. Assignments within the range of individual abilities and available time are more frequently completed. The cooperative interest of parents should be cultivated, so that pupils will be encouraged to complete home study.

3. The actual class participation

Time should be allowed for class contributions on the basis of assignments. Time should be divided judiciously so that there can be wide participation. Each contribution should be related to the overall lesson emphasis. Carefully tying together the work of various pupils enriches each part. Sharing discoveries of well-prepared students benefits all.

C. Discussion

The discussion method produces pupil reaction by requiring interpretation of the lesson. This prevents the pupil from merely acquiring knowledge without appropriating it. It aids in a continuous development or gradual construction of the lesson and stimulates the spirit of inquiry and personal interest. No other method is as well adapted for securing individual expression or application of the lesson. This method can be expanded to include such emphases as the panel discussion and other group methods.

Having started a discussion, it is necessary to direct it along the line of the lesson. The discussion will develop as pupils and teacher react and interact under proper guidance. Some pupils may manifest major interest in minor items. Overtalkative pupils may want to monopolize the time, not giving opportunity to the reticent, retiring person who needs experience in expression. In spite of these problems, discussion or conference is the most nearly ideal of all teaching methods. It encourages expressional activity and leads pupils to form their own judgments rather than to accept passively or to reject unthinkingly the message of the lesson.

D. Project

The project method which has been used successfully in the public schools in recent years can be used effectively in Christian education. A project is essentially a purposeful activity which the student plans because he is interested in it. He gathers information about it and carries the project to completion.

The project should have teaching value as well as practical application. Usually the project is started in the class period, but can be completed during the week at home.

The project method gives the pupil opportunity to learn by doing. Cooperation, tolerance of others' opinions, initiative, responsibility, alertness, and judgment are developed. The project method strengthens character and provides opportunity to acquire and develop skills.

The research project helps to make the pupil an independent investigator. Here the teacher assigns each pupil a part of the lesson to investigate for himself. During the lesson period, class members present their reports. These are commented upon, evaluated, and organized under direction of the teacher. This method is especially effective for adolescent and adult classes. Successful reporting strengthens the value of the research.

1. Reports should be brief

Ask members of the class to participate briefly in order to allow enough time for a summary of the findings.

2. Reports should be correlated

Curiosity will be aroused, interest sustained if the reports fit into each other. The teacher can accomplish this by making suitable assignments and distributing them to the best advantage.

E. Lecture

The lecture method has long been used by many teachers. It permits the teaching of a large class and allows close adherence to the teacher's planned presentation. It provides an uninterrupted, connected discourse, leading up to a pre-determined conclusion. Both time and effort are saved, since no time is wasted getting to the point or waiting for slow-responding pupils. There is no danger of being side-tracked by an unexpected suggestion from the class. The lecture method permits smooth, easy, direct, and systematic development of the lesson.

All these advantages, however, are lost if the class does not follow the lecturer and think with the teacher. Some pupils will take no thought of the lesson during the lecture and do nothing about it afterward. Mental, spiritual, and physical growth come through activity and this can be insured only when the pupil contributes to the development of the lesson.

This method requires thorough preparation, since the effectiveness of the lecture depends upon the careful use of material, illustrations, and supporting evidence. In the actual lecture, the teacher must avoid rambling. He must vary his manner, speak clearly, use the language of the pupils, lead the minds of the pupils in the discovery and solution of problems, insert good illustrations and examples, use humor occasionally, and watch for audience reaction in order to gauge his lecture to it. If the class size and teaching situation permits, he should intersperse his lecture with pupil reactions, comments, questions, and discussions. This will increase the interest and stimulation and will accomplish the teacher's purpose.

Suggested Questions for Review

1. Why are aims and objectives essential to teaching?
2. What should be the threefold aim of the church leader and teacher?
3. What is the major responsibility of a Sunday school teacher?
4. Why is storytelling an effective method of teaching?
5. Discuss the major principles in good storytelling.
6. List basic principles for effectively using recitation in teaching.
7. Contrast the advantages and disadvantages of the discussion method.
8. What are the values of the project method?
9. What are the advantages of the lecture method?
10. What caution is necessary for effective use of the lecture method?

Additional Exploration

1. Examine Sunday school quarterlies for various age groups and note what aims and objectives are stated.

2. Visit a Sunday school class in session. Find out beforehand the aims of the lesson. Throughout the session, observe the teacher's methods and procedures to fulfill these aims.
3. If you are presently teaching, list the specific changes that you desire in the lives of your students. In a brief, specific manner, transpose this list into aims and objectives to keep in mind as you teach.

> *"And he gave some . . . teachers: For the perfecting of the saints for the work of the ministry, for the edifying of the body of Christ: Till we all come in the unity of the faith, and of the knowledge of the Son of God, unto a perfect man, unto the measure of the stature of the fulness of Christ"* (Ephesians 4:11-13).

CHAPTER THREE

How to Teach

It is an old axiom that "teachers are born, not made." Present-day educators, however, believe that many so-called natural gifts may be in reality acquired habits. Of course, some people do have more teaching gifts than others. Teachers who are guided and corrected by recognized principles of pedagogy, who are enthusiastic about their task, who love their pupils, and are thorough in their preparation can be assured of success.

This philosophy does not minimize the work of the Holy Spirit. Every Sunday school teacher ought to live the surrendered life and to be guided by the Holy Spirit. The Holy Spirit is not dishonored by the application of the laws of teaching any more than He is dishonored when we comply with the laws of gravitation.

Our Lord Jesus Christ consistently observed the laws of teaching and learning. These principles can be observed, evaluated, and catalogued because they are inherent in man's make-up. "All things were created by Him (Christ), and for Him, and He is before all things, and by Him all things consist (Colossians 1:16, 17). "In whom (Christ) are hid all the treasures of wisdom and knowledge" (Colossians 2:3).

The *Seven Laws of Teaching* by John Milton Gregory, first published in 1884, constitutes an excellent standard and sets the pattern for the work of a teacher.

> "A clear and simple statement of the important factors governing the art of teaching, it has been especially successful as a handbook for Sunday school teachers. In recognition of Dr. Gregory's great service to the University of Illinois, two members of the School of Education undertook the revision of his book in 1917. Dr. William C. Bagley and Warren K. Layton made every effort to retain both the form and the substance of the original, making only those changes suggested by the recent developments in educational theory and practice."[1]

Gregory (1822-1898) was an outstanding educational leader. He was a district school teacher at the age of seventeen. Later he became a Baptist minister. He was, however, soon recognized as an educator of superior abil-

---

[1] John Milton Gregory, *The Seven Laws of Teaching* (Michigan: Baker Book House, 1954), p. 3.

ity. "After serving as state superintendent and as a college president in Michigan, he labored for thirteen years in laying the foundation of the University of Illinois. He has earned a secure place in the history of American education."[2]

> "From the early twenties to the middle forties, there was among academic psychologists a de-emphasis upon the importance of attention and a general neglect of it."[3] Hence, a disagreement with Dr. Gregory. "But today attention is quite generally considered to precede and to be an integral component of perception."[4]

> "For a short time, also, there was a tendency to discredit the learning of facts and to emphasize 'personality development' . . . We now recognize that the home and school have a vital role to develop the child intellectually . . . (They) must furnish the tools for thinking as well as develop skills in using these tools."[5]

Attention is concentrated consciousness and facts are tools for thinking. Both are exceedingly important for all real learning.

The revision and reprint of Dr. Gregory's book was welcomed by many evangelical teachers who recognized the abiding values of the theories and principles so clearly presented in it.

THE LAW OF THE TEACHER   A *teacher* MUST BE ONE WHO KNOWS THE LESSON OR TRUTH OR ART TO BE TAUGHT.[6]

Some leadership education courses give more attention to the *methods* of the teacher than to the *message* of the Word of God. This can be dangerous unless the teacher is thoroughly familiar with *what* is to be taught. Methods and message are both important. For this reason, one-half of the teaching units of the Certificate Courses of Evangelical Teacher Training Association are devoted to the direct study of the Bible and related subjects. (See FOR YOUR INFORMATION, pages 94, 95.)

In secular education, a knowledge of the subject is essential. In Christian education, it is important that the teacher know the Word of God. Knowledge is the material with which the teacher works. Imperfect knowledge will be reflected in imperfect teaching. What a man does not know, he cannot teach. *"Know thoroughly and familiarly the lesson you wish to teach,—teach from a full mind and a clear understanding."*[7]

Miss L. Flora Plummer, in *The Soul-Winning Teacher* says:

> "In our study of the Scripture, we should strive to be thorough. We should dig deep; the best jewels are mined far below the sur-

---

[2]*Ibid.*, p. VIII.
[3]O. A. Roback, editor, *Present Day Psychology* (New York: Philosophical Library), p. 114.
[4]*Ibid.*, p. 313.
[5]*Ibid.*, p. 112.
[6]Gregory, p. 5.
[7]*Ibid.*, p. 6.

face. Accuracy is always in demand. The bookkeeper's columns must be correct to a cent. The carpenter's joints must fit exactly, else his work is but a botch. Each lesson thoroughly mastered gives added power for the next, but every lesson skimmed over only weakens us for that which awaits us in the future. The difference between success and failure, between feebleness and power, is that of invincible, persistent determination on the one hand, and lack of energy and a yielding before difficulties on the other."

The teacher should know *more* than he has time to teach, not just enough to fill in the time. This requires earnest study and investigation in order to have a grasp of the complete lesson. The teacher who masters his subject can be at ease as he directs the class in its thought and active participation.

THE LAW OF THE PUPIL A *learner* IS ONE WHO ATTENDS WITH INTEREST TO THE LESSON.[8]

Long before Spurgeon became a great preacher, he was a successful children's worker. In his instructions to his teachers he said: "Get the children's attention. If they do not hearken, you may talk, but you will speak to no purpose whatever. If they do not listen, you go through your labors as an unmeaning drudgery to yourselves and your pupils too. You can do nothing without securing their attention."

"Gain and keep the attention and interest of the pupils upon the lesson. Do not try to teach without attention."[9]

A. Attention

Cradle Roll, Nursery, and Kindergarten children have only brief attention spans, perhaps one minute for each year. Usually no more should be expected of them. Primary department children will have an increasingly lengthened period of sustained attention. They begin to appreciate their own abilities and to enjoy longer periods of thought or discussion. By the middle of the first grade or during the second grade, well-trained public school pupils begin to make the transition from so much physical activity to the enjoyment of mental activity. Their attention span becomes noticeably lengthened. At any grade level the wise teacher seeks first to gain the attention, then to retain it, and finally to turn attention into interest.

1. Uncontrolled or passive

This attention is of the "flitting" kind and may be distracted by any circumstances that arise. The mind is not sufficiently fixed on the lesson to prevent the eye or the ear from being subject to outside attractions.

2. Disciplined or active

---

[8]Gregory, p. 5.
[9]*Ibid.*, p. 6.

Attention may be compelled by an appeal to the will power of the pupil or by certain disciplinary measures. In the Sunday school, however, it is unwise to exercise discipline in order to enforce attention. Yet Dr. George Herbert Betts in *How to Teach Religion* says, "The child must be trained to give attention. He must be taught to maintain an attitude of attention, not allowed to become listless and troublesome the moment his interest is not held to the highest pitch."

3. Absorbed or secondary passive

Pupils learn most readily when they are so "absorbed" in their study as to be oblivious to what is going on around them. Disciplined interest often develops into absorbed interest as a result of effort or persistence. Both the teacher and the pupil may contribute to such a mental attitude.

B. Interest

Attention is dependent on interest. It is easy to gain and hold the attention of an interested pupil. An imperative command or some clever eye-catching trick may temporarily attract attention, but genuine interest alone will sustain it. As Dr. Goodrich C. White suggests: "We must find a way to give boys and girls things to do that seem worthwhile to them so that they will crowd other things out of mind."

Ability to gain and maintain interest will depend on:
1. Discovering the pupil's plane of thought.
2. Guarding against outside distractions.
3. Providing a lesson suited to the pupil's capacity.
4. Enlisting the pupil's co-operation in the lesson.

THE LAW OF THE LANGUAGE   The *language* USED AS A MEDIUM BETWEEN TEACHER AND THE LEARNER MUST BE COMMON TO BOTH.[10]

The teacher with his important equipment of knowledge is on the one hand. The pupil with his requisite of interested attention is on the other. The next step is to set up successful communication between them.

The teacher may have a larger vocabulary than the pupil, but he must limit himself to the language of the latter. If the teacher fails or refuses to adjust to the pupil's language, the instruction will not be comprehended. *"Use words understood in the same way by the pupils and yourself—language clear and vivid to both."*[11]

The language will differ for every age and department in the Sunday school. To this end Gregory suggests that the teacher:

A. Study constantly and carefully the language of the pupils
B. Express himself as far as possible in their language

---

[10]*Ibid.*, p. 5.
[11]*Ibid.*, p. 6.

C. Use the simplest and fewest words that will express his meaning
D. Use short sentences of the simplest construction
E. Explain the meaning of new words by illustrations
F. Test frequently the pupils' understanding of the words he uses

THE LAW OF THE LESSON THE *lesson* TO BE MASTERED MUST BE EXPLICABLE IN THE TERMS OF TRUTH ALREADY KNOWN BY THE LEARNER—THE UNKNOWN MUST BE EXPLAINED BY MEANS OF THE KNOWN.[12]

This law deals directly with the lesson or truth to be taught. It is fundamental to all pedagogy. *"Begin with what is already well known to the pupil upon the subject and with what he has himself experienced,—and proceed to the new material by single, easy, and natural steps, letting the known explain the unknown."*[13]

All teaching must begin at a known point of contact. If the subject is entirely new, then a known point must be sought. This law of association or contact is basic for all mental development. New truths can be understood only in terms of the old.

Our Lord was a master of this law. He constantly built new truths on well-known facts. His hearers were familiar with the Old Testament. His crucifixion was to be similar to the lifting up of the brazen serpent in the wilderness. His burial and resurrection were likened to the experiences through which Jonah had passed. The times of His return would be like the days of Noah and the days of Lot. Future events were portrayed in terms of things that had already happened.

To observe the law of the lesson, the teacher should be aware of several related procedures.

A. Contact with former lessons

What has already been studied may be assumed to lie in the realm of the known. If the teacher has taught these former lessons, he will be on familiar ground with his pupils. Every review is a demonstration of this law, and those who emphasize reviews best observe this principle.

B. Proceed by graded steps

An athlete never sets his mark at an unattained height and then tries to jump it. He starts at a level which he can clear and then advances inch by inch until a new height is established. So a pupil must fully grasp each truth before the next can be explored and understood. New ideas become part of the pupil's knowledge and serve as a starting place for each fresh advance. More rapid progress can be made and higher achievement attained if the teacher observes this principle.

---

[12]Gregory, p. 5.
[13]*Ibid.*, p. 6.

C. Illuminate by illustration

The illustration is "a retreat to familiar ground." When the advance is too rapid for the mind to follow, temporary retirement to known scenes permits the understanding to catch up. Figures of speech, such as similes, metaphors, and allegories have sprung out of the need for relating old truths and familiar scenes and experiences to the new lesson.

THE LAW OF THE TEACHING PROCESS *Teaching* IS AROUSING AND USING THE *pupil's* mind TO GRASP THE DESIRED THOUGHT OR TO MASTER THE DESIRED ART.[14]

"There can be no religious integration of the self until the thinker or learner himself is involved in his thought."[15] The pupil should assimilate every portion of the Bible as he is fed. The teacher's activity is not effective until he applies the spark of interest and produces action in the pupil. *"Stimulate the pupil's own mind to action. Keep his thoughts as much as possible ahead of your expression, placing him in the attitude of a discoverer."*[16]

"The highly personal business of fitting your child to utilize his capacities to the fullest is the direct opposite of the assembly-line process."[17] If pupils do not think for themselves, there will be little lasting result. The learning processes are quickened when pupils become independent investigators. It is true that knowledge can be obtained without a teacher, and some successful, self-made men have never attended schools of higher learning. This does not, however, eliminate the necessity for schools and teachers. The good teacher simply provides favorable conditions for self-learning. He does not merely impart knowledge. He stimulates his pupils to acquire it. He motivates his pupils and sets an example of earnest, serious scholarship. He leads, but he does not stand in the way of his pupils' progress.

A. Provide thought material

Mental processes are limited to the field of acquired knowledge. The pupil who knows nothing cannot think—he has nothing to think about. In order to compare, criticize, judge, and reason, the mind must work on the material in its own possession. For that reason, the pupil needs factual information which will serve as the basis of thought. Education is in part a drawing out process, but no teacher can draw out knowledge that has not been previously implanted in the pupil's mind.

---

[14]*Ibid.*, p. 5.
[15]Cecil De Boer, *Responsible Protestantism: The Christian's Role in a Secular Society* (Grand Rapids: Wm. B. Eerdmans Pub. Co., 1957), p. 230.
[16]Gregory, pp. 6 and 7.
[17]H. W. Dodds, *Public Schools in Crisis.* Ed. by Mortimer Smith (Chicago: Regnery Co., 1956), p. 67.

B. Ask questions

Man's mind is stirred by asking ceaseless questions about the world and the universe. An object or event that excites no question will provoke no thought. Questioning is not merely one of the teaching devices; it is the heart of teaching. It excites self-activity. It leads to the discovery of truth. It sets the wheels of the pupil's mind working.

C. Provoke investigation

Even more than asking questions, it is important to arouse the spirit of investigation. Rich educational processes begin when pupils ask, "Who, What, When, Why, Where, How?" The maturing mind grapples with the problems of the universe. The falling apple caused the inquiring mind of Newton to ask the question of gravitation. The boiling teakettle propounded to Watt the problem of a steam engine. The question is both an index to the pupil's mind and an index to his inner self. His question leads to self-realization and self-seeking. The teacher should stimulate this natural quest for knowledge, as well as a natural desire for expression.

THE LAW OF THE LEARNING PROCESS

Learning IS THINKING INTO ONE'S OWN UNDERSTANDING A NEW IDEA OR TRUTH OR WORKING INTO HABIT A NEW ART OR SKILL.[18]

The effective teacher arouses and guides the self-activities of his pupils. He also evaluates the pupils' response to the teacher's efforts. He helps them to evaluate new truths and translate them into the arts and skills of basic daily living.

Learning requires active interest and attention, and a clear and distinct act or process which only the pupil can perform. He must cultivate his own mind by his own power to achieve a true concept of the facts or principles of the lesson. This law of the learning process is vital.

Contrary to general opinion, the work of education is more the work of the pupil than of the teacher. We can learn from others but true learning is more than repetition. Original discovery is a thrilling, stimulating process. The discoverer borrows facts known to others and adds that which he has learned by experience. The teacher uses this law to guide the pupil to be an independent investigator.

There are three distinct stages of learning, each one carrying the pupil toward the mastery of learning.

A. Reproduction

"Require the pupil to reproduce in thought the lesson he is learning—thinking it out in its various phases and applications till he can express it in his own language."[19] It is possible to reproduce the exact words of any

---
[18]Gregory, p. 5.
[19]*Ibid.*, p. 7.

lesson by committing them to memory. This is all that is attempted by unskilled pupils, or required by teachers who have a poor concept of the learning process. The pupil who does not understand what he has memorized does not *possess* the lesson. He is like a man who purchases a book and places it in his library, but makes no use of it.

B. Interpretation

There is a decided advance in the learning process when the pupil is taught to give more than the actual words or facts that he has learned. When he expresses his own opinion of these facts, he understands what he has been taught. He has learned to deal with his own thoughts as well as the thoughts of others. Failure to insist on original thinking is a most common fault of untrained teachers. A good teacher seldom asks the question, "what?" This calls for only factual answers. A trained teacher uses the word "why," so that the pupil learns to think—to think for himself.

C. Application

Education is more than the acquisition or understanding of knowledge. No lesson is fully learned until it is applied to life. Knowledge is power—but only when it is conquered, harnessed, put to work. Expressing an opinion may exercise the mind, but applying knowledge affects the will and transforms the life of the learner. If practical, personal application is neglected, Sunday school pupils will be "always learning, but never able to come to a knowledge of the truth" (II Timothy 3:7). This kind of so-called learning is mere "head knowledge" and does not result in the life-changing, transforming operation of the grace of God.

THE LAW OF REVIEW AND APPLICATION THE TEST AND PROOF OF TEACHING DONE MUST BE THE REVIEWING, RETHINKING, REKNOWING, REPRODUCING, AND APPLYING THE MATERIAL THAT HAS BEEN TAUGHT.[20]

Business sessions are usually opened with the reading of the minutes of the previous meeting, and closed with the minutes of that day's proceedings. There are reviews of what transpired—at the beginning and end of the meeting. The first review establishes close relationship with former sessions. The second carries the day's proceedings into the next assembly. It is important to make contact with former lessons at the beginning of each lesson. It is equally essential that each day's instruction be carried over to the next lesson, and that all learning be vitalized in the lives of the pupils. "Review, review, REVIEW, *reproducing the old, deepening its impression with new thought, linking it with added meanings, finding new applications, correcting any false views, and completing the true.*"[21]

This law involves a knowledge and practice of three areas of emphasis.

---

[20]*Ibid.*, pp. 5 and 6.
[21]*Ibid.*, p. 7.

A. Strengthen and perfect knowledge

Review is more than repetition. New lessons and fresh topics are seldom completely understood. They may distract the attention and their novelty may dazzle the mind. The first viewing of a picture will not reveal every detail. The second reading of a book usually brings out facts that were missed in the preliminary perusal. So it is with Bible study. No other book needs more careful reading and study. No other book is so filled with treasures and blessings. A review of familiar, favorite passages will reveal new light and disclose new lessons.

B. Remember and confirm knowledge

Review familiarizes and strengthens through association of ideas. A person who is introduced to a group of people may not be sure of many of the names. Later, when another stranger is presented, he will "catch" additional names and his memory will be strengthened. The lesson that is studied only once will soon be forgotten. What is repeatedly reviewed will become part of the equipment of knowledge and be permanently remembered and used. This is the correct measure of achievement.

C. Apply and practice knowledge

"Practice makes perfect." Frequent, thorough review renders knowledge readily useful. The Scripture texts which help us most are those which have been applied and used. These verses are remembered when occasion demands. Truths which have become familiar by repetition shape conduct and mold character. If we desire to have great truths sustain and control us, we must practice them until they become habitually fixed in our lives. The "line upon line and precept upon precept" rule of the Bible is a recognition of this truth.

Review is important, necessary activity; it is an essential condition of all true teaching. Not to review is to leave the work half done.

Suggested Questions for Review

1. How can teachers be assured of success in teaching?
2. What is the law of the teacher?
3. How does one apply the law of the pupil?
4. Name and distinguish between the three kinds of attention.
5. Upon what four things does the ability to gain and maintain interest depend?
6. List at least five ways in which the teacher can observe the law of the language.
7. Illustrate Christ's use of the law of the lesson.
8. In what ways does a good teacher advance self-learning?

9. Why is factual knowledge basic to teaching and learning?
10. Why is questioning sometimes called the heart of teaching?
11. Discuss the three distinct stages of learning.
12. Define the law of review and application.

Additional Exploration

1. Observe some outstanding teachers both in the church school and public school. Inquire of them what laws and principles of teaching they utilize. Compare and contrast with the laws discussed in this chapter.
2. Read a biography of a successful teacher. What factors apparently made this teacher successful? Evaluate these according to the laws discussed in this chapter.

NOTES

CHAPTER FOUR

Instructional Aids

An "AID" is not an end in itself—a crutch upon which poor teachers may lean. It is a means for improving instruction. It combines the eye gate with the ear gate to create an impression. It is "any device that assists an instructor to transmit to a learner facts, skills, attitudes, knowledge, understanding, and appreciation."[1]

IMPRESSIONAL TEACHING AIDS Remedial reading experts report that some public school pupils fail because their teachers do not use the valuable material in the guides and manuals. They feel that the teachers should make fuller use of these aids in order to produce more logical thinking.

A. Teacher's manual

Since it is the primary purpose of the Sunday school teacher to affect the pupil's life by teaching the Word of God, there should be a consideration of the aids that will deepen impression. Both trained and untrained teachers will discover that the teacher's manual is a valuable help, if it is used wisely.

1. Use it with the Bible

In lesson preparation the teacher should first read the Bible lesson text and the related Scripture before referring to the quarterly. Good teachers use the quarterly, but do not limit their instruction to its contents. Evangelical Sunday school literature usually contains a background of Biblical reference material to give the teacher a broad basis for understanding.

2. Use it for the pupils

One little boy aptly described his Sunday school teacher as "a quarterly wired for sound." The teacher should emphasize the Bible, not the manual, to his pupils. The manual should never be allowed to come between the teacher and the pupils. It is even more important that it should not stand between the pupils and the Bible. The attention should be upon the Bible —the real textbook.

Ministering to pupils means meeting their deepest needs. The manual can help the teacher to understand his pupils and show him how Bible knowledge can meet present-day living problems.

---

[1]Kenneth B. Haas and Harry Q. Packer, *Preparation and Use of Audio-Visual Aids* (New York: Prentice-Hall, Inc., 1950), p. XI.

3. Use it out of class

The properly prepared teacher does not need to use his manual during the class period. Teaching from the Bible, he will remind his pupils of the inspired Source of Christian instruction. His very attitude toward the Book is his strongest means of non-verbal communication.

B. Audio-visual aids

Human communication is not limited to the spoken and written word. Recent studies show the value of audio-visual aids and the effectiveness of all the other non-verbal communications. Pupils who fail to grasp a truth through the ear gate may comprehend it through the eye.

A wide selection of audio-visual aids is available. The teachers who use them have reported increased interest, more constant attention, and more enthusiastic response. One teacher expressed it, "They never look puzzled when you show them pictures."

It is an accepted practice to distinguish between projected and non-projected audio-visual aids. *"A visual aid is any instructional device that can be seen, but not heard. An audio-visual aid is any instructional device that can be heard as well as seen."*[2]

1. Objects

Objects appeal to everybody. A small object such as a coin, stone, or paper may be used at any time. A scroll, for instance, will visualize the form in which the Old Testament was originally written. A homemade model of stocks will portray vividly the painful torture of Paul and Silas in prison (Acts 16:24). One teacher, while telling the story of Mary anointing the Lord in Bethany (John 12:1-8), took a bottle of perfume and poured some on her handkerchief until the room was filled with the odor. Another teacher, while discussing Hebrews 4:12, showed a double-edged dagger to his class.

These are valuable and effective teaching aids. They actually give the pupil firsthand experience with the thing that is being discussed. A well-equipped Sunday school should have a collection of Bible and missionary models and curios among its materials. However, any teacher as well as using descriptive words can find teaching aids in the commonplace things that are all around. Sanctified imagination will supply unlimited object lessons.

2. Maps

Maps help pupils become familiar with the topography and the locations of Bible countries and cities. Maps should be consulted frequently. The roll-up type is preferable, as it will take less space and last longer. The class should also have access to a globe, for locating mission fields and comparing the size and location of Bible lands with the pupils' own country.

---

[2]*Ibid.*, p. 11.

3. Pictures

"Skillful use of pictures has resulted in highly successful instruction, which proves that teaching may be done much more effectively by pictures than by words alone."[3]

Pictures are so readily accessible that teachers should use them freely. However, unless carefully planned, the pictures may become an end in themselves.

The Christian teacher should keep a file of good pictures, collecting them from various sources. A class may use several pictures to present a running narrative of the life of Christ, from His birth to the resurrection. Too much attention to the details of a picture will cause the pupils to remember it more than the lesson.

4. Chalkboard

Chalkboards are widely accepted as effective teaching aids. Every Sunday school classroom should have chalkboard (formerly called blackboard) space for use by teacher and pupils. Its great usefulness is to clarify the instruction by means of diagrams, outlines, and drawings built step by step. Even the action of the teacher helps to sustain attention.

A teacher need not be a professional artist. One teacher with a piece of chalk equals two teachers. A short line, a few stick figures, a circle or square—these will represent people or cities or events. New and difficult words, names of characters, important dates— all can be written down. An outline or summary can be jotted down. Avoid too much detail. At the board keep these five things in mind:

   a. Don't block the view.
   b. Write legibly, but quickly.
   c. Stand at the side of your work as much as possible.
   d. Talk while writing, but do not talk to the board.
   e. Use chart and graph presentations whenever possible.

5. Flannelgraph

The flannelgraph is a versatile teaching device. It has been widely used in the Sunday school, Vacation Bible School, Child Evangelism meetings, weekday classes.

It secures attention at the very outset and, as new factors appear, it sustains the interest. At the end of the lesson, the class may repeat the story, placing the figures upon the board. This combines the faculties of hearing, seeing, and doing.

Frank G. Coleman, in *The Romance of Winning Children*, says "there are three fundamentals that must be mastered if the flannelgraph is to be used successfully:

   a. Dexterity
      The skillful manipulation of the flannelgraph is 'attention getting.' This takes practice. The teacher should know the story

---

[3]*Ibid.*, p. XI.

and should practice telling it with the use of the flannelgraph. Everything 'must' be ready before the class session. The figures should be arranged in the order in which they are to be used. Keep the hands as free as possible. Let the story move rapidly. Talk while you work, but keep an 'eye contact' with the class.

b. Suspense

Curiosity is an important factor. Arouse pupil attention by the manner in which the figures are placed on the board. Keep the class in suspense. Hold attention until the last word has been spoken and the final figure is placed on the board. Do not place any material, except the background, on the board before you begin to speak. Develop the scene as you unfold the story and delay the final scene until the last possible moment.

c. Movement

If the teacher walks about as he tells the story with the flannelgraph, his movement will help to sustain attention. Every motion or gesture occupies the eye, and even though many may seem unnecessary, they will put life into the instruction."[4]

6. Projected visual aids

Years ago David Livingstone used a "magic lantern" to gain interest and friendship among the African natives. Modern slide projectors and motion picture projectors are much advanced over Livingstone's lantern. Today's projectors, either with or without sound track, are widely used in Christian education.

It is a simple matter to buy or rent individual slides, film strips, or motion pictures in color. For the Sunday school teacher, a projector can be a valuable supplement to instruction.

EXPRESSIONAL TEACHING AIDS A clear distinction must be made between aids for impression and aids for expression. Impression is related to the law of the teaching process. It involves all the teacher does to stimulate the pupil to mental activity. Expression involves the law of the learning process and requires the pupil to reproduce in expression the lesson he is learning—thinking it out in its various phases and applications till he can express it in his own language. The manner in which these activities of expression are employed is important in their utilization toward true learning. Expressional activities provide means for appraising true learning. Christ's words "Ye shall know them by their fruits" (Matt. 7:16) might well be interpreted to include the student's activities in times of expressional opportunities.

To be effective, the teacher must provide the kind of expressional activi-

---

[4] Frank G. Coleman, *The Romance of Winning Children* (Cleveland: Union Gospel Press, 1948), p. 146.

ties that involve careful thinking, reasoning, analyzing, evaluating, summarizing. This active involvement of the mind, heart, and will urges the students to become "doers of the Word" (James 1:22).

Expressional activities do not displace good teaching—they are good teaching. They are most effective because they supplement the personality and skill of the instructor, and they assist in student assimilation and application.

A. Importance

Audio-visual aids may help to reach and stimulate the pupil's mind. But even if he is well informed and is able to retain information, audio-visuals do not necessarily secure a response. Expressional aids are important for

1. Deepening the impression

"A little child will probably forget what he hears; he may forget what he has seen; he will not forget what he has done." Learning is a process of listening, looking, and doing. As a pupil expresses himself, he reimpresses his own mind and learns the truth through a different sense channel —not only through eye and ear, but now through his hand. Pupils *learn by doing*. Learning begins and continues in what the learner does. The pupil taking piano lessons receives certain impressions when the teacher demonstrates a musical selection, but he doesn't begin to learn until he practices it for himself. Without practice, there can be no real learning.

2. Capitalizing on energy

The best solution for discipline problems is keeping the active pupil occupied. His boundless energy and ceaseless activity need to be utilized. The wise teacher harnesses this activity and energy. He directs and controls it, but does not try to suppress it. Directed expressional activity can serve excellent educational purposes. Attempts to suppress it may bring disastrous results.

3. Reaching the personality

We have not actually contacted the personality until there has been the appropriation and application of knowledge. Our aim is the development of Christian character and training in Christian living. This is not basically the teacher's *instruction*; it is the pupil's *response*. But the teacher himself serves as the best visual aid. The pupils see in his life the ideal that they may attain. Unconsciously they imitate noble character and appropriate something more valuable than any instruction. To reach the personality, expressional aids must do more than provide "busy work" for restless pupils. The activities may have a positive value in shaping life.

B. Pupil's manual

The pupil's manual is an important expressional aid. It represents and sets the pace for the pupil's response to instruction. This manual is only a means to an end and not an end in itself. The teacher whose primary concern is that his class should show neat, orderly manuals is defeating his ultimate purpose.

No lesson series is complete without pupils' manuals. In fact, they can be as important as the teacher's manual. It is preferable that the pupil's manual be studied and completed at home. On this foundation, the teacher can build an educational superstructure. Some teachers do not give careful consideration to these all-important manuals. The books may be carelessly given out, with only a casual suggestion that they be studied at home. The good teacher solicits the co-operation of the home, the church, the school, without which there will be little or no preparation.

Under certain circumstances, part of the class period may be used for supervised study. Written work provided in the book can be done at this time. Many teachers use this method with splendid results. They observe the pedagogical principle that teaching is "getting a response."

For children above Kindergarten ages, every pupil's manual should include:

1. Something to write

There may be blanks to fill in, sentences to complete. Writing helps the pupil to record his knowledge and provide for a personal response to instruction.

2. Something to find

The pupil who is required to search the sources for an answer will be likely to remember the information. His activity will make an impression upon his personality and develop his initiative for the discovery of truth.

3. Something to draw.

The lesson will be strengthened if the pupil draws a map, chart, graph, or picture. This "handmade" drawing need not be artistically correct or complete.

A map of Palestine may show the boundaries, Mediterranean Sea, Sea of Galilee, Jordan River, and Dead Sea. The pupil can locate and print the names of several important cities. These are the basic geographical factors for a study of the life of Christ. Other items can be added as the story develops.

C. Handcraft

Years ago Marion Lawrence stated that "a child remembers 10% of what he hears, 50% of what he sees, 70% of what he says, and 90% of what he does." What a pupil discovers and writes and draws and constructs will be indelibly impressed upon his mind. But in all probability he will best remember what he constructs.

The Sunday school hour is too brief for extended work in manual arts. Some teachers believe that manual expression provides only "busy work," but it has been proven that pupils do not waste time if their constructions are correlated with instruction. Handcraft may also be used during pre-session activities.

1. Materials

Many inexpensive materials are available for handcraft projects. These include paper, pasteboard, plastic and plaster of Paris. A Bible-times village can be constructed entirely of paper, cloth, and wood.

2. Projects

A resourceful teacher will use projects that are related to one lesson, or to a lesson series. The ETTA textbook on Vacation Bible School* provides many practical helps for teaching in the church school.

A class will learn more by constructing a model of the tabernacle than by reading the Exodus "blue print" a hundred times. Making a relief map of Palestine will teach more about the mountains and valleys than by reading about them, or even by special instruction in Bible geography.

Finally, aids for expression can strengthen the spiritual life of the pupil. The teacher utilizes classroom activity as a means of making impressions more vivid, more permanent, more vital, and more appealing. Properly correlated activities will develop Christian character and Christian living.

Suggested Questions for Review

1. Define a teaching aid.
2. Describe ways to use a teacher's manual profitably.
3. Define audio-visual aids.
4. Appraise the value of audio-visual aids for communicating truth.
5. Give some examples of how objects can make a Bible lesson become alive.
6. List several suggestions for using the chalkboard effectively.
7. Discuss three fundamental principles for using flannelgraph.
8. What are the values of a good pupil's manual?
9. State reasons for using handcraft as an expressional aid in teaching.

Additional Exploration

1. Distinguish between impressional and expressional teaching aids. Visit a class during the week and determine the proportion of class time spent for each type. If you are teaching, have someone observe your division of time. Discuss the effectiveness of this proportion and suggest changes which could improve this arrangement.

---

*Mrs. Ruth C. Clark, *Vacation Bible School* (Wheaton, Ill.: Evangelical Teacher Training Association, 1959).

2. Check your local Christian bookstore, publishers' catalogs, and community resources to discover what is available in both impressional and expressional teaching aids for a particular age group. List those aids which are relevant to an immediate, intermediate, and long-range teaching program. This can be an individual or group project. Data could be recorded and classified and available to the entire church teaching staff.
3. Clip handcraft ideas from magazines, newspapers, and other *how-to* publications. File according to age groups. Suggest ways these can be utilized as instructional aids.
4. Read through one of the Gospels and chart the various methods Jesus used in His teaching.

CHAPTER FIVE

Gathering Lesson Material

"The greatest need in our church work today is trained teachers who put their whole mind into their preparation, their whole soul into their presentation, and their whole life into their illustration." This philosophy of Marion Lawrance strikes hard at teachers who are satisfied with a hurried preparation on Saturday evening for Sunday's lesson. A trained teacher knows that he needs preparation. Poise cannot be maintained in the presence of the class without mastery of the lesson and a reserve knowledge of Bible truths. Dr. A. H. McKinney, in *The Top-Notch Teacher,* writes:

> "Are we not seeking to learn how the teacher may have that poise during the lesson study period which gives him the mastery of the situation? It may not be easy to gain such poise, but it is well worth paying a large price in order to obtain it. What is the price? Prepare carefully every lesson you are to teach. Get the largest possible acquaintance with the contents of the Bible as a whole, with its historical, geographical, and social background, with the truths which it imparts. Having done this, you will have made much progress toward the poise which is so desirable and so essential in successful teaching."

Full preparedness calls for definite plans. Definite plans demand properly selected materials. The teacher's selection of materials will be governed by the needs of the pupils. And the pupils' needs will be manifested in the teacher's close intercourse and acquaintance with them.

The resourceful teacher "finds tongues in trees, books in the running brooks, sermons in stones, and good in everything."

SOURCES OF MATERIAL **A. Bible**

The Bible is the teacher's major source, his primary line of defense. It is the recognized text of the Sunday school. It is the inspired Word of God.

The Bible is its own best interpreter. A comparison of Scriptures with Scriptures will throw light on obscure passages. But there are many valuable supplementary materials that will help the Bible teacher to master the Word of God.

1. Information

2. Some Bibles contain valuable notes: geographical, historical, and archaeological helps. More complete helps may also be purchased in separate volumes. *The ETTA Library for Christian Educators* provides helpful information and lists many suggested textbooks.

2. Interpretation

Some Bibles have notes and comments on various passages. In such, a commentary is provided with the text. These explanations have real value, especially to teachers who have not had specialized training. Commentaries, however, should not be accepted as the final, complete answer. Commentators may vary in their opinions. The use of several reliable commentaries will provide a cross section of interpretation.

3. Investigation

Good teachers will help their pupils become independent investigators. That is impossible unless the teachers develop their own abilities and techniques of investigation. A reference Bible will help both teachers and pupils to locate parallel passages and other materials that illustrate the truth which is being studied. Pupils will acquire real skill in using their Bibles during class sessions.

B. Bible dictionary

A Bible dictionary is in reality a topical Bible, gathering from the entire Scripture every reference pertaining to a particular subject.

C. Bible concordance

An exhaustive concordance gives helpful references for practically every word in the English Bible. It also lists terms from the original writings and includes a comparison of variations in revised versions. Strong's, Cruden's, or Young's complete concordances are widely accepted.

D. Bible commentary

After a careful and prayerful investigation of the Scriptures, the teacher may consult Bible commentaries for interpretations and explanations of difficult passages. Reliable, up-to-date commentaries are written by recognized Bible scholars who are abreast of recent developments in Biblical literature and archaeology. These volumes should be available in every church library.

E. Teachers' manuals and other lesson helps

In studying his lesson, the teacher reads the Bible, first for the story; second, for the incidents; third, for the persons mentioned; and fourth, for its doctrinal and practical teachings. After a background of independent research, the teacher finally consults manuals and other lesson helps. He has already discovered many things mentioned in the lesson helps. But he has the satisfaction of blazing the trail for himself.

GATHERING LESSON MATERIAL 43

Lesson helps should supplement the teacher's knowledge. They should be used *with* the Bible, never as a substitute for it. Any teacher who uses lesson helps exclusively is apt to do little original thinking.

Helps can clarify difficult passages, provide apt illustrations, and supply essential information on ancient manners and customs. The teacher should use Bible-centered, Christ-honoring lesson helps, so that he may obtain a right understanding, interpretation, and application of the Scripture.

F. Maps

Sunday school pupils need to be familiar with Bible geography and history. The journeys of the patriarchs, the wanderings of Israel, or the campaigns of Joshua and David cannot be followed without the use of maps. Small maps, conveniently located in most Bibles, are helpful. Wall maps are much more practical and profitable, especially if constructed by the members of the class.

G. Pictures

Christian educators recognize the value of visual education. Pictures may be used to present and illustrate the truth vividly. The greatest works of art depict Bible scenes. Hundreds of originals are on exhibition in art galleries. Whenever copies of masterpieces are available, they may be used. Selected and correlated pictures may be purchased in series for Sunday school use.

H. Other sources

There are innumerable sources for enriching Sunday school lessons: life experiences of teacher and pupils; current events in magazines, newspapers, bulletins, radio, and TV. Public schools, colleges, and other state agencies have audio-visual libraries. Manufacturers and distributors offer valuable audio-visual equipment and supplies, often free of charge. The local public library, travel agency, and the U.S. Government can furnish vital information.

How is this related to assembling lesson material for Sunday school? The teacher who is up-to-date on current affairs, who knows his subject thoroughly, and who understands his pupils will teach from the overflow of his rich life. Being resourceful, he will encourage resourcefulness in his pupils.

SELECTION OF MATERIAL "Go to the Bible for all things; to books for past things; to newspapers for present things; and to human nature for a point of contact." The teacher like a newspaper reporter should be on the alert for material. In his devotional study, in his reading of books, magazines, and newspapers, in listening to the radio and

TV, and in every personal contact, he should be gathering material for long-range lesson preparation.

A. Plan for future lessons

Carefully planned curriculums are not composed of independent, unrelated units. Each lesson is related to those preceding and those following. Taken together, they can develop a complete theme. Each day's study must be related to the general theme for the entire quarter.

To assure full, active class participation, the teacher must make assignments not later than the previous Sunday. This cannot be done unless the teacher has given considerable time to long-range planning and study. Consideration of future lessons is both practical and essential if the teacher is to have an effective ministry.

B. Provide for the needs of individual pupils

As materials are selected, the teacher should be aware of the needs of the entire class. He should also keep a clear focus on the individual members of the class. As a fond father searches for a personal gift for his son, so the teacher will be alert for materials to meet the needs of each pupil. This "personal touch" will enrich each lesson and each pupil. And, individual class members will be encouraged to "study to show thyself approved unto God" (II Timothy 2:15).

C. Meet the personal needs of the teacher

The trained, consecrated teacher realizes the importance of reading selectively, systematically, and intelligently. He knows that he can help his pupils only in the proportion that he is tapping reservoirs to enrich his own spiritual growth. As he extends his own vision, increases his own knowledge, deepens his own spirituality, and vitalizes his own faith, his pupils will drink from "rivers of living water" (John 7:38) rather than stagnant pools.

ACCUMULATING MATERIAL The human mind rarely remembers half of what it sees or hears. Psychologists claim that 90 percent of the ideas entering the mind are soon forgotten. One eminent educator believes that most ideas are lost in the first 24 hours. Provision should therefore be made for gathering and conserving worthwhile materials.

A. Paint mental pictures

The teacher who can present facts vividly will appeal to the imagination of his pupils. But he cannot show his pupils what he himself does not see. Ninety percent of imagination is memory. For this reason, lesson material should be reproduced in mental pictures. During his preparation, the

GATHERING LESSON MATERIAL 45

teacher should stop frequently, close his eyes, and form vivid pictures of the scenes and persons about whom he has been reading. This will develop his ability to visualize and will make his teaching more imaginative. Constant practice will enable the teacher to see new pictures vividly and to develop a "sanctified imagination,"—and his pupils will receive permanent impressions.

B. Provide a notebook

Writing helps the memory to retain information and preserves it for future use. Recording and filing materials make them available. Such a depository of teaching materials will be increasingly helpful.
  1. For general information
        "I thought a thought, but the thought I thought
        Was not the thought I thought I thought.
        So when next a thought I think I think—
        I'll write it down with pen and ink."
  Never read without thinking—never think without writing. The teacher who finds something worthwhile should copy it in his notebook or make a notation of the subject, book, and page, so that it can be quickly located when needed. The notebook should include the following information.
    a. Facts
    Statistics are valuable. They form a foundation and a strong court of appeal for class discussion. Quotations from representative leaders and educators carry authority. Information about the latest discoveries and inventions is useful as a point of contact with a wide-awake class.
    b. Experiences
    Human interest stories are fascinating. Many are related to the spiritual realm. Answers to prayer. Reports of God's providence. Demonstrations of God's power. Missionary adventure. These are most effective, especially if they are related to some class member or generally known as current news events. All pertinent information should be recorded correctly, including names, dates, places, sources of information.
    c. Illustrations
    Teachers need a large fund of stories and other illustrative material. Daily living is full of illustrations, but unless notes are made at the time, they will soon be forgotten. By taking notes and referring to them during lesson preparation, it is possible to have current, captivating illustrations for every lesson.
  2. For specific lessons
  The teacher's notebook is valuable in planning for future lessons. The teacher can survey the entire lesson series and strengthen each lesson. If he faithfully uses his notebook, he will soon come to regard it as one of his chief pedagogical aids.
    A 13-page notebook with one page for each lesson of the quarter will be

helpful. Amos R. Wells believed that there should be at least fifty-two pages, one for each lesson of the year. He says:

> "Head each page with the title of the lesson and the Scripture reference, and use these blank pages for planning your teaching far ahead. If you are a wise teacher, you will be always on the lookout for teaching material. Every walk through the woods gives you a teaching parable. Every copy of the newspaper gives you an illuminating incident from current history. Every book brings you a fine anecdote or appealing thought. Every day your observation of the men and women around you is rich in illustrative material. Much of this is entirely unsuited to the immediate Sunday school lesson, and will be lost unless you have this storehouse in which to garner it, placing it under that lesson with which it seems most appropriate."

C. Build a file

Starting a file is easy. It will enrich every teaching experience. Materials can be accumulated for use in the months and years to come. Seasonal themes can be highlighted—Christmas, Thanksgiving, and Easter. Pictures, object lessons, and other visual aids can be added. Assembling and filing material can mean real success in teaching and learning.

> "Some have not trouble in thinking out sermon outlines, locating information in their library books or remembering apt illustrations. If you are gifted in this way you may not need a filing system. Most of us have limitations in remembering things that we read, experience and hear about, and thus a system of filing is helpful. Consider your present needs and keep in mind the needs of the future as you decide on the method that you will use. Many have started a system and found that it worked well up to a point but because it was not expendable it became more of a burden than a blessing.
>
> "Generally, you should be able to understand the index that you plan to use. Sometimes better understanding is acquired after using an index but the general principles should be clear before you start."[1]

Suggested Questions for Review

1. Name and discuss at least seven sources of lesson material.
2. What types of supplementary guides do some Bibles have?
3. Outline a good procedure for studying the Bible lesson.
4. Why should lesson helps be used?

---

[1]Don Wardell, *Practical Help for Christian Workers* (Winona Lake, Ind.: Don Wardell, 1957), p. 44.

GATHERING LESSON MATERIAL 47

5. What caution should be exercised in the use of lesson helps?
6. For what purposes must all lesson material be selected?
7. Why are needs of individual students to be considered in the selection of material?
8. Why must the heart and mind of the teacher be prepared?
9. How can the teacher develop personally and thus improve his teaching?
10. What are the values of using a notebook for general and specific information?

Additional Exploration

1. Begin now to keep a notebook as suggested in this chapter. Be faithful in recording illustrations, experiences, and facts that will provide teaching material for the future.
2. Collect informational and inspirational material and classify according to subject matter and age level. Keep in mind your immediate, intermediate, and long-range needs. Incorporate materials suggested in chapter 4, projects 2 and 3. Include pictures, poems, articles, and statistics.
3. Select another Gospel to trace Jesus' use of various methods and objects in His teaching. (See chapter 4, project 4.)

CHAPTER SIX

Organizing the Lesson

Poor teachers are satisfied that lesson preparation is complete when they have enough material to "fill in the time." This is not enough—teaching is more than simply "keeping going."

Sunday school sessions are as important as public school sessions. Sunday school teachers have much to learn from successful school teachers who painstakingly prepare each lesson. An old adage states, "In the teaching of every class someone must suffer. If the teacher does not suffer before the lesson, the pupils are apt to suffer afterward."

Lesson material needs organization. There must be elimination as well as accumulation. A teacher may not teach every detail of an assigned lesson, but he should complete all that he planned. Well organized, carefully outlined material will fit into the lesson period so that every precious moment will be turned to the best advantage.

HOW TO ORGANIZE MATERIAL   Dr. George Herbert Betts in *How To Teach Religion* describes four different plans commonly used in preparing material for teaching.

A. The haphazard plan

This is really no plan at all. It is, however, common among Sunday school teachers who lack both training and ability.

B. The logical arrangement

This consists of sorting and selecting relevant material. Different parts are fitted together logically—proceeding from the known to the unknown. This produces logical thinking on the part of the teacher and his pupils.

C. The chronological approach

Large portions of the Bible can best be grasped and retained when presented in their historical relationship. God's revelation to man was chronological. In each age He revealed more of His divine purpose to chosen writers who "spoke as they were moved by the Holy Spirit" (11 Peter 1: 21). Chronological organization is related to the preparation of each lesson and to the entire curriculum of Bible study.

D. Psychological programming

This method consists of planning the subject matter to fit the comprehension and experience of the pupil. Why teach truth, however significant and profound, if it is beyond the comprehension of the pupil? Material must be adapted to the understanding or it is soon forgotten. Even if retained, it will be dull and uninteresting.

Both secular and Christian educators stress the psychological organization of materials. This method must not, however, be permitted to deemphasize the Bible content of instruction. There must be a balanced emphasis on both the application and the acquisition of God's Word. It is true that we dare not "forget the child" when we teach. It is equally true that we dare not forget the Bible—the only authoritative revelation of the truths of Christianity. The use of Bible-centered material does not imply that the Sunday school ignores the age and understanding of the pupil.

All teaching material should be tested for its grading to the age and understanding of the pupil. However, we do not need psychological tests for God's Word. It is, in its entirety, the Word of God, and that which may be too advanced for one age or one stage of Christian development can be taught in another.

STEPS IN ORGANIZING MATERIAL

A. Aim of instruction

All preparation will center around the aim or purpose of the lesson. Curriculum materials should be examined in the light of this purpose. The teacher should ask, "What can I find here to meet the need of my pupils?"

The teacher's quarterly will probably suggest a general aim for the series and specific aims for individual lessons. Do not be limited to these aims. The writer's suggestions may be set up to fit the *content* of the lesson, but the teacher adapts the lesson to the needs of his pupils.

Does the lesson teach faith, obedience, love, duty to God and man? Does it stress the Christian graces of humility, kindness, generosity? Is Bible study, prayer, Christian fellowship encouraged? Does it present and explain the "call of God" for Christian service at home or abroad? Does it deal with the Gospel—God's plan of salvation? The teacher should constantly direct these truths to reach and affect each member of the class. He should be constantly aware of individual needs. Specializing in the individual will help to determine the teacher's aims and provide dynamic motivation for his method and application.

B. Methods employed

Margaret Slattery in *Talks with the Training Class* says:

"There are three pathways by which we may approach every human life—feeling, knowing, willing. From one to seven years, the child is a slave to his feelings . . . Seven to fourteen is the period when reason and knowledge are important . . . Fourteen to twenty-one is the period of the will. When heart and brain and hand are open to serve the world in the best way, then ideal developement has taken place."

Many factors enter into the decision about methods to be used. These include the pupil's age and the content and extent of the material. A good teacher will vary the method and the type of the material for more effective presentation. More material is needed for a lecture than for discussion. More time is required for student reports and assignments. If questions are to be used extensively, less material can be covered.

All these factors have an important bearing in determining what kind and how much material can be used. The character of the lesson will also determine its treatment. For example, the conquests of Joshua or the journeys of Paul will require extensive visual instruction.

C. Materials used

After determining the aim and method, the teacher should study all the available helps. Not all lesson helps can be used. The teacher must select that which will help in the realization of his aim.

After years of teaching experience, Amos R. Wells wrote:

> "Learn to simplify your teaching and focus it more upon a few facts and truths. As I remember it, I used to put enough into each half hour for two full hours. The result must have been to confuse my pupils and fill them with dismay. My teaching was all lectures, though usually under the thin disguise of questions and answers. Thus I was all the time pouring into baskets full of holes. If I had to do it over, I would think less of what I was giving, and more of what the pupils were getting."

Plan enough time for reports, assignments, questions, Bible memory work, pictures, and other collateral material. All these materials contribute to well-rounded lesson development.

D. Lesson outlined

Trained, experienced teachers may prepare their own outlines of material and procedure. Inexperienced teachers may prefer to use outlines suggested in the teacher's manual. With study and experience, however, all teachers can soon learn to construct their own outlines and lesson plans.

An outline should include the general divisions or topics with minor points, illustrations, and applications grouped under each.

The ease, effectiveness, and conclusiveness with which the lesson is taught depends largely on the clarity of the outline. Facts should be listed in the order of their importance under the topic or division to which they are related. The teacher can easily pre-arrange the climax so that it comes in the concluding minutes. If there is insufficient time for every detail, he can cover the main heads of the outline, omitting some secondary topics. Following this plan, the teacher will not be caught by the closing bell.

E. The lesson plan

A lesson plan should be brief, simple, and practical. It will aid the teacher in directing and organizing his lesson. Preparing a good lesson plan will actually conserve time and effort.

The following is a suggested lesson plan. Notice that the steps necessary to a teacher's preparation have all been summarized and placed in this plan. The teacher may adapt this plan to his specific needs:

>Lesson title:
>Scripture:
>Memory verse:
>Central truth:
>Lesson aim:
>Teaching methods:
>Visual aids and other materials needed:
>Lesson outline:
>>Approach:
>>Body:
>>Conclusion:
>
>Possible assignments for the following lesson:
>My evaluation of this class session (to be filled in after the lesson has been taught):

F. Questions prepared

If the lesson is to be developed by the use of questions, the facts and truths should be brought into prominence, so that the pupils will recognize the train of thought and feel that they are making progress as the lesson proceeds.

Advance preparation makes it easier to formulate specific, thought-provoking questions that are pertinent to the lesson.

The best questions often result from the response of the pupils and therefore cannot be completely anticipated in advance. The teacher can inspire good participation by having a barrage of questions prepared.

G. Illustrations selected

Appropriate illustrations must be selected and included in the outline beforehand. Some teachers introduce the lesson with an illustration. This approach gains attention and sets the stage for the presentation. The opening illustration may be woven into the entire teaching period, especially at its close. Anticipate the points that will need clarification. Use illustrations from everyday experience, such as nature, history, stories, or songs.

H. Applications suggested

This important phase of preparation is not difficult for the teacher who has assembled and organized his material to meet the pupils' needs. Every teacher should ask this pertinent question, "How can I get my pupils to express in daily living the truths that I am preparing to teach?" As he prays and plans for the personal application, the Holy Spirit will enable the teacher to follow the right procedure.

I. Pupil's co-operation

This phase of preparation requires careful thought. Training pupils is more difficult than teaching them. It is easier to "teach" a pupil than it is to lead him to "learn" by his own study. The best teachers guide their pupils to become independent investigators of truth. Definite assignments for each pupil should be planned in advance. The desire for pupil co-operation will motivate the teacher to plan and make assignments.

1. Research projects

Research assignments may be made for the individual or group. They may be done as "homework" or by the group during the Sunday school session. In either case, assignments should be:

   a. Definite

It is not enough to urge pupils to "study the lesson." Even those who want to do this may be overwhelmed and discouraged by the bigness of the task. The teacher must communicate clearly, helping his pupils to know *how* to study and *what* to study.

It is also essential that the teacher suggest definite sources of help. Without proper guidance, pupils will not know what books to consult. Usually it is advisable to give them the material and offer to help them in research.

   b. Individual

Assignments should be personal and individual. One pupil may be given a question to answer; another, a topic for study and report; a third, a map to draw; a fourth, some Bible references to compare. The interest, capacity, and ability of each pupil should be considered in selecting the nature of the assignment. Every member of the class should be included.

2. Class reports

Pupils are frustrated if they do out-of-class assignments and then are not given opportunity to report their findings in class. The good teacher will plan for the presentation of all assignments, using various means to make these effective.

   a. Questions

In the preparation of the questions, the teacher who knows the interests of the pupils will "draw them out" to express themselves freely.

   b. Topics

Where the class has a good background of Bible knowledge or is making an intensive or extensive study of the lesson, individual pupils may use their assigned topics to introduce general discussion. Members of the class will usually participate in any discussion which they have introduced. Failure here may hinder full co-operation. Even timid or backward pupils will be drawn into the class activities, under the skillful leadership of a trained teacher.

c. Student teaching

In older classes, it is sometimes profitable to have one of the pupils teach the lesson. This experience for the student teacher should be carefully supervised, so that each class member will have a genuine learning experience. The teacher should brief the student teacher before the class session. During a post-session evaluation the student teacher may be encouraged to pursue training courses and thus qualify for future service in the Sunday school.

Suggested Questions for Review

1. What is the difference between assembling and organizing lesson material?
2. What is the value of a well-organized lesson?
3. Discuss four methods of organizing material.
4. Describe the steps in organizing material.
5. What factors determine the aim of the lesson?
6. What factors determine the methods to be used?
7. How does one determine the amount of material to be used?
8. Discuss the outline of a good lesson plan.
9. What provision should be made for homework?
10. What plans should be made to involve all pupils in class participation?

Additional Exploration

1. Study and evaluate published Sunday-school lessons to become more familiar with the principles of good lesson planning. Notice especially the lesson outline.
2. Write a Sunday school lesson for presentation, applying the principles of gathering and organizing lesson material as outlined in this chapter. Choose a lesson you will use in the future.

CHAPTER SEVEN

Effective Illustrations

The skillful teacher knows how to manipulate one of the most valuable implements of instruction—the illustration. The illustration is a retreat to familiar ground. It constitutes an important application of the law of apperception. "The pupil can learn the new only in terms of the old." When the advance is too rapid for the mind to follow, an illustration is introduced as a temporary retirement to known scenes so that the pupil's understanding may catch up with the teacher's progress.

VALUE   The teaching value of illustrations cannot be overemphasized. Most successful preachers and other speakers know the art of illustrating. All Sunday school teachers should realize the effectiveness of illustrations and cultivate their skillful use.

The teacher's work is not done when he has presented the facts of a lesson. These truths must be placed within his pupil's capacity, or little progress will be made.

It was not Spurgeon's remarkable voice nor his depth of thought so much as his vivid illustrations that enabled him to hold multitudes spellbound. The use of illustrations by such an eminent preacher should prove their value. The Lord Jesus Christ in teaching adults used many illustrations. How often did He say, "the kingdom of heaven is like unto . . ."? He recognized that new instruction needed the illumination of the light from familiar scenes. How frequently He referred to nature and human life to clarify His instruction!

A striking object lesson was necessary before Peter could understand that God did not want Peter's old prejudices to stand in the way of his ministry to the Gentiles (Acts 10:9-26).

The Old Testament also presents an impressive array of illustrations used by the prophets!

Jeremiah used the girdle, the bottle, and the potter's vessel; Ezekiel, the roll, the tile, the beard; Amos, the locust, the plumbline, the summer fruits; Zechariah, the myrtle trees, the measuring lines, the candlestick.

These Biblical illustrations justify modern day use of this device as an important part of the teacher's equipment. However, a word of warning is needed. Even though illustrations are important, their value is lessened if they are overdone. Sometimes a story is so vividly told that it is remem-

EFFECTIVE ILLUSTRATIONS 55

bered but the truth forgotten. Use striking illustrations that will recall the truth. Do not use those that are simply remembered for the interest they arouse. Too many illustrations may confuse perception and hinder thought.

VARIETY The sources of illustrations are almost unlimited. The observant teacher finds them in everything he sees or does. And there is almost no end to the ways in which they may be used in teaching. There are, however, two general divisions:

A. Visual

We are so accustomed to think that "Sunday school teaching is talking" that it is necessary to re-emphasize the fact that pupils receive and remember what is directed to the eye gate and that they comprehend such instruction easily and quickly.

  1. Objects

It is one thing to use an object for study. It is vastly different to use it for illustration. Whenever a pupil's eye rests on some object related to the truth to be conveyed, the dubious look on his face gives way to the smile of comprehension.

When Christ placed a child in the center of the group, the little one did not become the subject of discussion, but the striking illustration of humility. As Christ taught about the kingdom of heaven, He said, "Behold, a sower went forth to sow." As His "school" assembled by the Sea of Galilee, He referred to the "fishermen casting their nets into the sea." Out in the countryside, He said, "Behold the fowls of the air," and "Consider the lilies of the field." The shepherd and his sheep illustrated and inspired many of Christ's most familiar and valuable lessons.

  2. Pictures

Not all classes have access to the living objects that characterize a good teacher's instruction. Time and distance may prohibit the direct use of these things. But pictures and photographs may be substituted. What words cannot convey, the picture may communicate.

  3. Models

Models of the ark, the temple, and oriental houses will convey truth more readily and accurately than verbal descriptions. Drawings and diagrams are invaluable. With all age groups the teacher can use a chalkboard to advantage.

  4. Maps

Maps always help to visualize locations, especially in lessons that involve the movements of the characters. Large wall maps are valuable for conveying a correct estimate of situations and distance.

B. Verbal

When verbal illustrations are used, they must be in clear, simple language. They should employ the actual, useable vocabulary of the pupils. Words and phrases that are familiar to the hearers will not distract them but will help them to grasp the truth.

1. Stories

Spurgeon suggested that there is nothing like stories to command interest and to relieve dullness of perception. D. L. Moody used fascinating incidents to make his messages clear. The illustrations in his sermons are excellent, and his printed messages have attracted millions, largely because of his ability to recast truth in story form.

a. Bible

The Bible is the best source of verbal illustrations. Bible stories convey the truth as God intended. They are God-given lessons in themselves.

b. Life

Next to Bible stories, the best illustrations come from everyday life. Real life stories should be told vividly, faithfully portraying the details but not sacrificing the truth. In his enthusiasm to paint a colorful picture, the teacher must not exaggerate. Stories which contain improbable details quickly lose their power and interest.

2. Parable

Parables must be distinguished from stories. Our Lord had a larger purpose in view by their use.

a. To clarify truth

Jesus seldom defined the doctrines He proclaimed. An example of this is the kingdom of heaven about which He taught so frequently. To His hearers, its deepest meaning was not fully understood. Christ did not give a formal definition. He did reveal its character by comparisons which were familiar to his listeners. Matthew thirteen records the seven comparisons He used.

b. To conceal truth

Our Lord expressly declared His motive when the disciples asked why He spoke in parables (Matthew 13:10-13). To His enemies, His words were but an innocent story. To the disciples, the parables were filled with significant meaning.

c. To stimulate thought

Jesus did not always furnish an interpretation of His teaching. For some parables He gave the key (Matthew 13:18-23, 36-43). His illustrations provoked thought and aroused the spirit of inquiry which He satisfied when He was alone with the disciples.

3. Comparisons

Making comparisons is one of the easiest and simplest uses of illustration. As pupils grow in knowledge and experience, this method becomes proportionately successful. It is interesting to note how frequently Christ used comparisons. He declared, "I am the bread of life"; "I am the living water"; "I am the Good Shepherd"; "I am the vine, ye are the branches." He called His disciples "the salt of the earth," "the light of the world."

4. Allusions

Older pupils may be appealed to by allusions to historical, biographical, literary, and scientific data. This time-saving device provides food for thought and stimulates the pupils to study in order to understand the meaning implied. The scholarly Paul used similies and metaphors to explain nearly every spiritual truth in the Christian life. Undoubtedly Paul was familiar with law, medicine, teaching, architecture, warfare, agriculture, commerce, Greek games, and seafaring life. He referred to all these in his teaching.

ILLUSTRATIONS THAT LIVE What makes an illustration vital? Why do some illustrations sparkle with interest? Why do others fall flat?

It is important that teachers understand the right use of an illustration. To be effective, an illustration must have several characteristics.

A. Brevity

Illustrations are "windows to let in the light." They are "scaffolds to be used in erecting a building." They must be long enough to convey the truth adequately, but brief enough to allow the pupil to absorb the teaching. Beyond this, an illustration may become "excess baggage."

B. Newness and freshness

Illustrations "wear out" by repetition. When pupils say, "We've heard that one before," they lose interest in the lesson. Using the same illustration to teach various truths may cause confusion instead of clarity. Effective illustrations can be drawn from current events and daily experiences. Their freshness will appeal to every wide-awake pupil.

C. Aptness

There are some illustrations that do not illustrate. If there is no likeness or only a faint resemblance between the illustration and the instruction, nothing is accomplished by its use.

D. Clarity

Sometimes the teacher may use an illustration that is not as familiar as the instruction to be clarified. Illustration about an oasis, a plain, a desert, or mountain would mean little to anyone who has never seen these places. Even the thought of God as Father may not be clear to a child who knows nothing of a father's love in the home.

On the other hand, illustrations that are too simple excite contempt. If they are too complicated, they will not be grasped. These extremes will be avoided by the teacher who knows his pupils—their school attainments, home life, desires, interests, and spiritual development.

E. Dignity

Poor illustrations degrade the truth and debase the hearer. They lead the thought into entertaining, less hallowed regions. Too many humorous illustrations will weaken the teacher's influence. Illustrations that lack dignity will spoil the presentation and explanation of solemn truths.

No Sunday school teacher should ever stoop to the use of questionable stories. There is an old adage that says, "If it's doubtful, it's dirty." Purity of life and thought must always match purity of doctrine.

Lester B. Mathewson, in his splendid textbook on *The Illustration* provides a self-correcting course, covering the origin and use of illustration. He lays down several important principles:

1. Never talk down to boys and girls. They resent a patronizing manner.
2. Everything you say must be within the range of their experience or understanding.
3. The teacher's manner must be friendly and sympathetic. Children want to know first of all if you understand their life, their ambitions, troubles, and ways of looking at things.

> "A wisely chosen illustration is almost essential to fasten the truth upon the ordinary mind, and no teacher can afford to neglect this part of his preparation."—HOWARD CROSBY.
>
> "Be understood in thy teaching, and instruct to the measure of capacity—Precepts and rules are repulsive to a child, but happy illustration wins him."—TUPPER.

Suggested Questions for Review

1. To what important law of teaching is the illustration related?
2. Give examples of illustrations employed by several Old Testament writers.
3. Name four types of visual illustrations and state the value of each.
4. Show how our Lord used objects for purposes of illustration.
5. List various types of verbal illustrations and their values.
6. For what purpose did Christ use parables?
7. Name five requisites for a vital illustration.
8. Discuss several important principles in the use of illustrations.

Additional Exploration

1. Start a file of illustrations, classified according to subject and age level. In evaluating illustrations to be filed, keep in mind the principles outlined in this chapter. Or incorporate this material in the file suggested in chapter 5, project 2. This may be an individual or group project.
2. Ask three Sunday school members to tell you what lessons taught during the past year they best remember. Inquire to what degree illustrations caused this lesson to be remembered. Be prepared to relate to the group for evaluation as to the function and nature.

CHAPTER EIGHT

Asking Questions

The question is a teaching device that can be most powerful and effective. It is an art—one of the fine arts—which when once acquired will be the making of a teacher. Dr. Herman Harrell Horne says, "The interrogation point is the badge of the teaching profession." Francis Bacon declared that "the skillful question is the half of knowledge." The real test of a teacher is the *response* of the pupils. His questions must not only instruct, but educate—lead out his pupils. The response of the pupil will depend on the skill with which the question is used.

The Gospel accounts record more than one hundred questions—startling, unusual, unexpected questions. The Lord Jesus Christ was a master of the art of questioning. At the age of twelve He was asking questions (Luke 2:46). At the beginning of His public ministry He asked His first two disciples, "What seek ye?" This is typical of the thought-provoking and reflecting character of all His questions. Even in His preaching He frequently asked, "What think ye?" and "How think ye?" A study of our Lord's questions is in itself a course in teaching techniques.

Anybody can ask questions. But not everybody can ask questions that really teach. There is little or no value in reading questions from a quarterly and asking the pupils to respond with the printed answers. Such a method deadens the pupils' interest in the Bible and creates an aversion to the lesson hour.

WHY ASK QUESTIONS To appreciate the value of good questions, the teacher must understand their purpose. Questions provide a most important stimulus to the mind. Education becomes effective when pupils begin to ask questions. The question serves many purposes.

A. To awaken interest

The teacher must make contact with the pupils in order to arouse their interest. A question, carefully worded to strike the mind of the pupils, is like a fisherman's bait on a hook. It catches the interest and elicits immediate, spontaneous response. It stimulates the pupil's imagination and focuses his immediate interest on the lesson, thus providing the teacher with an alert, wide-awake class.

B. To direct thought

After a contact has been established, each succeeding question should move toward the goal which the teacher has set. Stimulated by questions that have unity and purpose, the pupils can be successfully directed from one area of thought to another. The question method will clarify the truth and lead the pupils to evaluate all available information. Class participation will be enriched because the pupils express their personal judgments, interpretations, and applications of the lesson.

C. To quicken participation

Whenever a pupil's mind has wandered, it can be recalled by a question. In an atmosphere of dullness, thinking becomes sluggish. A well-aimed barrage of questions will put new life into the class. Questions with life and vivacity will assure satisfactory progress. They should be asked quickly and answered just as speedily. If they cannot be answered by one, they should be passed rapidly to another.

D. To drive home the truth

Pupils may discuss a Bible truth without associating it in any way with themselves. The teacher must lead them to apply the truth to their own lives. A good question can accomplish this. Christ illustrated this when He asked His disciples, "Whom do men say that I the Son of man am?" When they responded, He quickly applied their thought by the personal question, "But whom say *ye* that I am?" (Matthew 16:13-15.)

PREPARATION OF QUESTIONS Reading printed questions from a quarterly will hide the teacher's personality and deaden every attempt at teaching. While this is true, no instructor can hope to frame his questions advantageously after coming to class. Pupils will not participate in the lesson if the teacher lacks skill in the use of questions. Good teachers prepare their questions in advance. In the preparation of questions, several different types should be studied and used.

A. Contact questions

Attention and interest can be aroused if the teacher begins the lesson with an appropriate contact question. The most familiar and frequent expression of Jesus was, "What think ye?" Conversations were introduced by inquiries such as, "Will ye also go away?", "Whereupon shall we liken the kingdom of God?", and "Whence shall we buy bread that these may eat?"

B. Rhetorical questions

Preachers and teachers often ask questions without expecting an answer. Such inquiries are asked for effect rather than reply. They occasion surprise and issue vital challenges. They stimulate mental activity.

Study the questions recorded in the Sermon on the Mount (Matthew, chapters 6 and 7). "Which of you by taking thought can add one cubit unto his stature?" "Why take ye thought for raiment?" "Why beholdest thou the mote that is in thy brother's eye?" "Do men gather grapes of thorns or figs of thistles?" Such questions do not demand answers. They require action.

C. Factual questions

The easiest questions are those that can be answered by information previously given. The reply fixes in the mind the instruction that has already been imparted, and, since the work of a teacher is not complete until it has been tested, factual questions reveal how much instruction has reached its goal. A good teacher is concerned that his pupils have many opportunities to reproduce the lessons they have learned.

D. Thought-provoking questions

Teaching is more than "hearing lessons." Questions must do more than test the pupil's knowledge. They must help the pupil organize and apply his knowledge. They should stimulate the pupil to know more and to think for himself.

In court a witness is subjected to examination and cross-examination. His own counsel will ask questions to direct his replies and stimulate his thoughts. In other words, the witness' own case can best be furthered by permitting his counsel to think for him. The opposing lawyer, on the other hand, does not ask leading questions. Instead, he compels him by the most rigid examination to do his own thinking. The witness will have to give all diligence to the barrage of searching questions if his replies are to be accurate and consistent. While his own counsel may *direct* thought, it remains for the opposing attorney to *provoke* thought.

A good teacher in order to stimulate his pupils will not only examine, but cross-examine them as well. He will prepare thought-provoking questions that involve:

1. Purpose

The word "what" elicits information; "why" determines purpose. A direct appeal to the reasoning faculties of the pupil will encourage independent thought. Our Lord demonstrated this approach many times. For instance, He struck at the consciences of His critics when He asked, "Is it lawful to do good on the sabbath day, or to do evil? to save life, or to kill?" (Mark 3:4). "Why call ye me, Lord, Lord, and do not the things which I say?" (Luke 6:46).

2. Opinion

Questions calling for personal judgment are more valuable than those that ask for "statement of fact." Pupils must learn to determine relative values. Personal judgment was encouraged by our Lord's questions, "What

ASKING QUESTIONS 63

thinkest thou, Simon?" (Matthew 17:25) and "Why callest thou me good?" (Matthew 19:17). Many of His questions were used to strengthen faith, "Wilt thou be made whole?" (John 5:6); "Believe ye that I am able to do this?" (Matthew 9:28); "Whosoever liveth and believeth on me shall never die. Believest thou this?" (John 11:26).

3. Application

The most thought-provoking question is that which leads to a practical, personal application of truth. A lawyer seeking a debate raised the neighbor question (Luke 10:25-37). Christ answered with the story of the Good Samaritan and asked the lawyer's opinion as to which of the three strangers was a true neighbor. The lawyer's reply called forth the divine dictum, "Go, and do thou likewise." In an entirely different situation Christ asked Peter the heart-searching question, "Lovest thou me?" and followed it by the command, "Feed my lambs" (John 21:15-17).

HELPFUL SUGGESTIONS The successful use of questions depends largely upon the way they are asked. The observance of the following principles will enrich the teacher, make his teachings more effective, and encourage the pupils.

A. Do not read questions

Questions must be asked, not read. Although previously prepared in writing, it is better to leave these notes at home. Manuscripts and notes are non-conductors of personal interest. Be independent of them, since they may come between the teacher and the class.

B. Avoid questions that reveal the answers

Some backward, bashful pupils may be encouraged to participate in the lesson by questions that suggest the answer. Such questions, however, have little power to elicit information or stimulate thought. Morever, they bore the wide-awake members of the class.

C. Avoid guessing questions

When questions can be answered by "yes" or "no," the pupils will be tempted to guess rather than to think. Whenever a pupil answers "yes" or "no," expect him to give a reason for his answer.

D. Avoid long questions or double questions

Long complex sentences are not easily retained. The pupil may forget the first part in his effort to grasp the last. Eliminate unnecessary words or phrases. State the question briefly. Involved questions are seldom necessary. They are nearly always confusing.

A small boy was being criticized for his answer to a teacher's question. He defended himself by saying, "Dumb question, dumb answer."

E. Ask definite questions

Indefinite questioning is usually the result of the teacher's failure to think clearly. If the question is not understood, the answer cannot be clear. Good questions are clear, simple, direct. Some questions may involve more than one answer. A pupil, hesitating between possible answers, will usually reply promptly if the question is restated clearly—and concisely.

F. Do not repeat questions and answers

If pupils know that every question will be repeated, they may develop the habit of inattention. Except for unusual circumstances, a question should not be repeated, but given to another pupil who is mentally alert. It is equally boring and time-consuming when the teacher repeats the pupil's answer after him. No pupil will put much life into his response if he knows that it is to be immediately reiterated.

G. State questions before assigning

Do not name the pupil or look at him while asking the question. When the question is stated first, all pupils will be attentive, since no one knows who will be asked to reply. This is one of the secrets of holding the attention of a class.

H. Assign questions judiciously

Never ask questions by alphabet or seating arrangements, for each pupil knows just when his turn will come. The element of uncertainty is a good incentive to alertness. Restless, disinterested pupils can be arrested by a timely question directed to them.

I. Encourage questions

A teacher's effectiveness is often revealed by the type of questions asked by his pupils. If class members have learned how to ask questions, it is because their teacher has stimulated them to search for truth.

An inquisitive mind not only indicates class interest—it reveals readiness for instruction. This is the index to the pupils' mental and spiritual development.

J. Answer questions with questions

An efficient, well-trained teacher answers one question with another. This throws the responsibility back on the pupil and makes him an independent investigator. Our Lord frequently silenced His critics in this way. When asked by what authority He taught and healed (Matthew 21:23-27), He agreed to reply if they could answer His question regarding John's baptism. This counter question placed the critics in a dilemma, and they were obliged to admit that they could not reply. For other examples of counter questioning, read Matthew 15:2, 3; 22:17-20; Luke 10:25, 26;

14:3-6; 18:18, 19. The Apostle Paul and the other early church leaders used this device. The catechetical method of instruction is an adaptation of this procedure.

Teachers usually ask questions to find out the extent of the pupils' knowledge. Pupils ask questions because they face difficulties which they wish to clarify. It is always effective teaching procedure to present a problem and challenge the class to find the answer. This is better than presenting the solution and then testing afterward to see if the pupils understand it. The wise teacher constantly stimulates the spirit of inquiry. He does not tell his pupils something they can find out for themselves.

Suggested Questions for Review

1. Give three examples of the Lord's use of questioning.
2. Discuss the value of good questions in the teaching-learning process.
3. List four types of questions and discuss the unique value and purpose of each.
4. Why should questions be prepared prior to class use?
5. What are the significant characteristics of thought-provoking questions?
6. Discuss the Lord's use of thought-provoking questions in His approach to individuals and to groups. Give two illustrations of each.
7. What is a key test in appraising a good thought-provoking question?
8. List six or more principles for the successful use of questions.
9. Why should a teacher encourage questions from class members?

Additional Exploration

1. Investigate Jesus' use of questions during any one period of His ministry.
2. Trace Paul's use of questions in Romans chapters 3 and 6. Classify these questions as to types.
3. Evaluate the suggested questions in the lesson helps of your Sunday school quarterlies. Classify these as to types and their uses. Compile a list of additional questions in conformity with the teachings of this chapter.

CHAPTER NINE

Teaching the Lesson

Effective Christian teaching is the result of the Holy Spirit's empowerment. But, the Holy Spirit is more likely to use the teacher who has a practical knowledge of good teaching techniques. Spirituality and correct methods are not mutually exclusive. Unless there has been careful, prayerful Spirit-guided preparation, teaching is likely to be fruitless. Study is prerequisite to effective teaching.

Training is essential. Christian educators know that teacher training classes, credit cards, certificates, and diplomas do not guarantee that teachers will be qualified for their work. Training does, however, provide a frame of reference. It establishes the basic knowledge, attitudes, and skills of the teacher.

APPROACHING THE LESSON PERIOD Specific preparation for any lesson will be more simple and efficient if the teacher is able to relate it to the steps outlined in the preceding chapters. The actual preparation and teaching of a lesson can be approached with confidence if the general aims, objectives, and principles of teaching are clearly understood. The resulting joy in teaching and the pupil's enthusiastic response will make this approach worthwhile.

A. Ready to begin

Prayer and preparation determine whether the teaching of a lesson will be drudgery or joy. For the well-trained, carefully-prepared teacher, each lesson is a satisfying experience. Having given adequate time, prayer, and thought to *planning the work*, the final step for the teacher is to *work the plan*.

B. Capitalize on the pre-session period

The campaign to win attention and interest begins before the first pupil arrives. The teacher ought to be in the classroom at least fifteen minutes early so that he will be able to extend a personal greeting as each member arrives. A teacher who is late is already at a disadvantage with his pupils. And the pupil's attitude is an index to his personal response toward the lesson and what the teacher may expect from him in the way of attention.

TEACHING THE LESSON

INTRODUCING THE LESSON The teacher's first sentences may determine the success or failure of the entire lesson. Upon the spirit and method of this opening attack rest the results that follow. The most carefully-made plans may avail nothing if the teacher fails in his approach to the lesson. The first concern is the *attitude* and *interest* of the pupils.

A. Contact with the class

The average pupil is likely to be absorbed with interests other than the Sunday school lesson. His mind is elsewhere. He is intent on other things, so that the lesson is approached with prejudice, if not with protest. How can the teacher create a right attitude? How can he win the pupil's confidence and attention? How make the transition into the plan of the lesson? If the pupil does not "attend with interest to the lesson to be learned," it is useless to proceed. Arousing genuine interest is the most successful method.

1. Current news events

The teacher may secure attention by referring to some current news. Older pupils read the newspapers and listen to the radio. They watch TV. They have a wide range of interests. Younger children will respond to any event related to their school or play. Teachers who are well informed and keenly interested in the weekday activities of the pupils will have no difficulty at this point.

2. Stories and illustrations

A well-told story can arouse and sustain attention. A picture or an object will gain immediate response. An illustration from everyday experience will attract attention and impress the truth which the teacher wishes to leave in the pupil's mind.

3. Reports of assignments

Pupils are interested in their own activities. Unless their homework has a definite place in the development of the lesson, it may be wise to begin the lesson with reports of completed assignments. The attention of the class can thus be directed to the significance and importance of homework, and the pupils can be recognized and commended for their reports.

4. Sustaining interest

Having gained the pupils' attention, the next problem is to hold it. The teacher should remember that the pupils' attention cannot be maintained without interest, and interest is never sustained unless the mind grasps the subject. The effective teacher will use every resource that is available in order to "hold attention" throughout the complete lesson period.

B. Contact with the lesson

In introducing the lesson of the day, it would be well to observe the following suggestions:

1. Relate it to previous lessons

Each new lesson is part of the overall curriculum of the Sunday school. It must be related to all preceding and succeeding lessons in order to interest the pupil and increase his understanding. The greatest human "life interest story" is revealed in the Bible. God's saving grace is also revealed. It will help to orient the pupil if he knows just what place today's lesson has in relationship to the entire story. Recent lessons, especially last Sunday's, should be carefully reviewed and associated with the day's lesson.

Review procedures should be varied and fresh. A teacher does not lose time by reviewing previous teaching. More real progress can be made in thirty minutes after five minutes have been spent making a point of contact, than in thirty-five minutes' effort to comprehend a disconnected lesson. But the review should not begin, "Boys and girls, last Sunday's lesson was. . . ."

2. Announce subject naturally

A formal statement of the topic is not necessary, but an interesting, informative, perhaps surprise presentation may grow out of the review period. The announcement of the topic of the lesson should attract as much attention as the headlines of a newspaper.

3. Announce objectives

Some teachers believe that it is wise to disclose their aims and objectives. Others insist that an application is more effective if the pupil is not warned in advance. Not all lessons need the same treatment. Handle each lesson differently. When there are temperance, missionary, or other special or seasonal lessons, the object of the lesson can easily be announced in advance.

4. Make the outline live

Like the lead line in a newspaper item, there is value in presenting a leading thought to stimulate interest in what is to follow. Sometimes an abbreviated, or even complete outline may be presented. However, if the teacher does not follow his outline, it would be a mistake to reveal it.

DEVELOPING THE LESSON "Well begun is half done." Having introduced the lesson, the teacher should proceed according to the strategy that was planned during his lesson preparation. The teaching of the lesson will reveal the extent and quality of his preparation.

As the teacher presents the lesson, he must remember that "one does not actually teach unless someone learns something." The best test is not what the teacher says, but what his pupils remember.

A. Stimulate the pupils to think

For this purpose the question may be most effective. The teacher who uses a series of thought-provoking inquiries will likely accomplish his purpose. Whenever information is imparted, the class should be expected to think it through with the teacher. *Good teaching* requires that the pupil be tested constantly to keep him alert and to see if he is profiting from the lesson.

Anyone who teaches through the use of questions must keep his outline clearly in mind. His pupils should be able to sense the development and progress of the thought patterns of the lesson.

As each point of the outline is developed, it is a good plan to sum up the results in positive form, and then proceed to the next step. Illustrative materials may be introduced by the direct statement of the teacher or by the leading questions of the pupils.

B. Reproduce thought

It is important that every pupil be stimulated to think. He must also be encouraged to express his thoughts. What the pupil expresses, he is most likely to remember. As Miss Plummer notes:

> "In all teaching it is well to use regularly the 'telling back' plan. Adults profit greatly by this method; with children it is essential. Never tell your class what you can induce them to tell you. Here is a common mistake. The teacher should use all his powers of diplomacy in getting a pupil to put into his own words that which his mind grasps. It is worth infinitely more to a pupil to tell some truth, even in a broken, bungling way, than to have you tell it beautifully and eloquently. When he can tell it, he knows it. He may hear you tell it many times without knowing it. Trying to tell it helps him to know it."

But in addition to reproducing the facts of the lesson—and this is the starting point—the teacher should help his pupil to express *himself*—give *his own* interpretation and *his own* application of the lesson. Because many teachers have failed at this point, some modern educators have overemphasized experience-centered lessons. But it is not necessary to remove the "truth" from its central place in order that pupils may do their own thinking. Pupils can be guided to experience Biblical truth.

C. Apply truth

The teacher should lead his class to face specific situations in which they need to practice the Christian ideal. This exercise will result in growth in grace. With constant emphasis on the application, as well as the acquisition, of knowledge—especially in the early years—pupils will learn and they will participate in each lesson.

When this procedure is practiced, the pupils will make application of the lesson to their choice of conduct, course of action, attitudes, and overall spiritual life.

Always remember that there is mental activity as well as physical. Self-expression may take the form of self-inhibition or self-restraint. Refusing to say or do what is wrong is none-the-less self-expression. Character is made up not only of impulses but also of restraints.

CLOSING THE LESSON The lesson should never end abruptly. Careful consideration should be given to a fitting conclusion to the lesson. The teacher should plan for three to five minutes for an unhurried and prayerful "drawing the net."

A. Summarize the lesson

The teacher's outline should include a summary of the lesson. Questions or class discussion may break into the planned outline, but the teacher should take time to sum up the net results of the class period, emphasizing the fundamental facts of the lesson. What are the important truths? What practical lessons have been taught? What final application should be made? How has Christ been revealed as the Saviour of sinners? How can the lesson be demonstrated at home, at school, at work?

B. Anticipate the future lessons

In teaching each lesson, keep the total objective in mind. Prepare the pupils for the truths that will follow in successive lessons. Let the pupils experience a panoramic view of the days and weeks ahead. Stimulate eagerness by whetting their learning appetites.

Before the class is dismissed, the teacher will call attention to next Sunday's lesson and present his plans for each student's participation in it. This is a good way to

1. Arouse interest

The teacher wants the class to come back next Sunday—and to come back enthusiastically. By some startling statement or striking question, curiosity and interest can be aroused. Authors usually conclude a chapter so that the reader can hardly wait for the next chapter of a serial story. In the same manner, an expert teacher will finish the day's portion of "the most interesting story in the world," with such a climactic ending that the entire class will look forward to next Sunday's installment.

2. Make assignments

Assignments must be carefully planned ahead of time, but the animated way in which they are assigned will determine the interest and enthusiasm of the pupils.

Suggested Questions for Review

1. List two guiding principles in approaching a lesson period.
2. Specify some ways to arouse interest in the lesson.

3. Suggest steps to take in introducing each lesson.
4. Why is it helpful to relate the lesson to previous and following lessons?
5. How can a lesson be developed?
6. How is reproducing the lesson related to applying the lesson?
7. How can the teacher lead his class to apply truth?
8. What should be included in closing the lesson proper?
9. What value is there to calling attention to future lessons?

Additional Exploration

1. Observe a number of classes where experienced teachers are in charge. Note their procedures in teaching. Endeavor to determine to what degree lesson procedure as presented in this chapter is followed.
2. Write a paragraph on problems and their solution related to one or more of the following topics:
    Arousing initial interest.
    Involving the class in participation.
    Handling those who like to monopolize class time.
    Making truths vital to the needs of the students.
    Motivating students to want to prepare for next class.
3. For an individual project, have a fellow class member evaluate your teaching of a Sunday school class. Let him base his judgment on all the principles that have been studied in this course.

CHAPTER TEN

Good Discipline

God is the author of law and order; Satan is the author of confusion and chaos. The words "disciple" and "discipline" come from a word that means "trained in orderliness." For this reason Christians are admonished, "Let all things be done decently and in order" (I Corinthians 14:40).

The Bible also teaches that "children are to be brought up in the nurture and admonition of the Lord" (Ephesians 6:4). Nurture is instruction, but admonition is discipline. Since the Sunday school is the training center of the church, its teachers and officers must not only impart instruction, they must also exercise discipline. If pupils are to learn to think, moral and spiritual development requires that they must be trained in orderliness.

Disorder interferes seriously with Sunday school. Effective teaching is impossible when a class is out of control. Disorderly pupils nullify the teacher's efforts. Instead of practicing obedience, reverence, and the principles of Christian conduct, they learn disrespect for the teacher and disregard for God's house, God's Word and God's day.

Children who are well behaved and obedient in public school may be disorderly in Sunday school. Why? Perhaps the teacher does not know how to express orderliness and Christian discipline. Perhaps he does not exercise the same authority as the public school instructor. He does, however, have the authority of God's Word. His authority in Sunday school is above that of public school. If the teacher lives a well-disciplined life, he will speak with authority. His manner and use of the Word of God will spell authority and will bring effective results.

SETTING THE PATTERN Order is contagious. So is disorder. One unruly pupil affects another; each distraction leads to another. A Sunday school superintendent or teacher with a poorly prepared program invites trouble. An orderly atmosphere in the Sunday school will command attention and respect. If chairs are properly arranged with songbooks in their places, the pupils will likely leave them that way. Books or papers on the floor extend an invitation for more to follow. An orderly atmosphere is conducive to orderly pupils. Teachers and officers should set a good example.

To stimulate good behavior, check the classroom equipment and procedures. If there are difficulties, they should be corrected. They include:

A. Discomforts

Classes should meet under favorable physical conditions. Pupils will not sit quietly if they are uncomfortable in chairs that are too large or too small. The result is wiggling, weariness, and unrest. Poor ventilation and extremes of temperature also contribute to discipline problems. Absence of coat and hat racks can also prove to be a disturbing element. Pupils ought to be as comfortable in Bible class as they are in the public school.

B. Distractions

There are many distractions which make it difficult for a teacher to gain and hold attention. Separate classrooms are the best guarantee that the teacher will have no rivals to contend for the attention of his pupils. Curtains afford partial privacy from visual distractions, but they do not completely obliterate sounds.

C. Disturbances

The superintendent should *protect* his teachers, so that they may teach their classes under the most favorable circumstances. Some officers interrupt the lesson to distribute offering envelopes or Sunday school literature or make announcements. These interruptions may upset the teacher, the class, and the lesson.

A superintendent should conduct a Sunday school as carefully as he operates his own secular business. All teachers should be guarded against intrusions and should be guaranteed sufficient time and privacy for their work.

EXAMPLE OF THE TEACHER

The pupil's conduct will be affected by the example of his teacher. The teacher needs to recognize this fact and give special attention to his own physical, mental, and spiritual life.

A. Appearance

A teacher should dress carefully, avoiding loud, flashy extremes in clothes. Hair should be carefully groomed. The entire appearance should be neat and clean.

Striking mannerisms or peculiarities will draw attention from the lesson and be an indirect means to disorder. The teaching rather than the teacher should occupy the pupil's thought. When this relative position is reversed, mental—if not moral—confusion follows.

B. Self-control

Most teachers hope that God will transform their restless boys and girls into quiet, attentive pupils, but few teachers pray for their own self-mastery. The Holy Spirit-controlled teacher is victorious. Even the most extenuating circumstances should not cause the teacher to lose control of himself. He who does not control himself is not likely to control others. Many things may try his patience, and he needs to be on guard lest he become irritated and impatient.

Pupils quickly discover if the teacher is in a state of confusion. As a result, they will disregard his leadership. To be effective, the teacher must experience the "fruit of the Spirit" and demonstrate the grace that makes pleasant and cordial relationship between teacher and pupil. The calm, quiet, forceful mastery of our Lord impressed His listeners and made them listen to His words. In every controversy He was master of the situation.

C. Instruction

The teacher must be master of his subject if he is to be master of his pupils. Miss Plummer says, "If there is disorder in the class, it is the teacher's fault. The lesson itself should keep order." The poorly-prepared teacher will have trouble. Orderliness in instruction leads to orderliness in conduct. Disorder leads to inattention and a lack of interest. A poorly-prepared teacher is always out of order.

ORDERLINESS OF THE PUPIL Disorder may be both intentional and unintentional. The first finds the cause in itself. The second results from some external cause. There are at least four general groups of disorderly pupils.

A. Thoughtless pupils

A public school teacher evaluates a home by the kind of child who comes from it. He recognizes the difficulty of neutralizing or lessening the influence of the home. The Christian teacher must be equally discerning. He should know which pupils are thoughtless—which are intentionally bad. Pupils may be taught reverence for sacred things, but if they are accustomed to disorder at home, it will be difficult for them to carry out their best intentions to comply with the teacher's wishes.

Many churches provide systematic training in the early years of a child's life. They believe that reverence for sacred things can be inculcated into his being and become a part of his life. If proper "conduct patterns" are formed in the Kindergarten and Primary departments, children will more likely be well behaved in the subsequent departments.

B. Restless pupils

Nervous tensions and frustrations are on the increase, even among Christians. Emotionally-disturbed children are not uncommon. The Sunday school teacher must help these children, and all the boys and girls who are naturally restless. Many Sunday school pupils come from homes where there is constant smoking, drinking, fighting, lack of affection, and deliberate disregard for the common decencies of life. Many parents "park" their children before a TV set from the time school is out until dinner time or even bedtime. Doctors advise against this because children need the sense of "belonging" to the family in its fellowship and recreation.

Teachers realize that in many TV programs the disconnected, flighty sequence works against their efforts to teach children to think logically. The Sunday school teacher seeks to counteract this evil, plus all the other unhealthy, unchristian impacts and allurements of today's world.

Parents should control these conditions, but many adults have become so accustomed to them that they do not realize their effect upon the impressionable minds of young children.

Public school teachers and Sunday school teachers who have learned to diagnose children's difficulties have an obligation to inform parents. Parental ignorance along these lines may be one factor in making America "the best half-educated country on earth."

It is true that "some boys don't go wrong because they don't go at all," and it is possible to be "so good as to be good for nothing." Robert Louis Stevenson said, "Give me the boy who has brains enough to make a mistake." The average child is an active creature. He delights in doing something. If his teacher does not keep him employed, he will supply his own entertainment. These wide-awake pupils need a full program of activities that will give them opportunities to participate in the lesson. Of course, the teacher must not overlook the "quiet" member of the class who also "earns by doing." Nevertheless, if good order is to be maintained, the active pupil will need a well-planned program of graded lesson materials and of expressional activities.

C. Self-centered pupils

The "spoiled" child always wants his own way. He is the center of attraction. His contribution seldom harmonizes with the lesson, and it is difficult to relate to the overall plan. Miss Plummer relates what one teacher did when an energetic pupil blew a whistle in class.

> "The teacher said, 'Why, Johnny has a whistle. A whistle is a very good thing. What is a whistle good for?' The interest of the teacher seemed so genuine that several were encouraged to reply, in spite of Johnny's red face. Then the application was skillfully made. The calls of the Bible, the warning, the admonitions were referred to as God's manner of attracting attention. Quick as a flash came the thought, the Bible says, 'Blow the trumpet in Zion'—a whistle blown for God's people, a warning we should all heed. The theme was developed helpfully. In the course of the diversion the teacher wanted to see the whistle, took it in her hand, commented a bit on its construction, and kept it until the completion of the lesson, in which are found some 'whistle warnings' of value."

Generally, the self-centered pupil will be reprimanded by the ridicule of others. Public opinion is a respected teacher. The child who always wants to be "it" will soon learn from his companions that selfishness and stubbornness may mean self-exile. For this reason, the self-centered child needs to be exposed to the leveling process of his playmates.

D. Malicious pupils

Relatively few children come to Sunday school to instigate mischief. If they are recognized by their companions as leaders, they can be real problems for the teacher. Activities and methods that work with other pupils may fail with these. Even a well-prepared and well-presented lesson may produce only limited response.

The teacher should not permit any unruly pupils to spoil the lesson period. He will have to be firm, yet loving, in dealing with this problem. He must never lose patience nor become indignant or sarcastic. To do so would reflect upon the character of the instructor and would accomplish nothing with the pupil. Kindness and firmness should be combined as the disorderly pupil is challenged, perhaps even reprimanded. If the admonitions are not respected, the pupil may be requested to withdraw. However, before such action is reached, the teacher should make several friendly contacts during the week. More than one "problem child" has been conquered by a persevering teacher who visited his home, discovered his interests, and won his confidence. "If any of you lack wisdom, let him ask of God, that giveth to all men liberally, and upbraideth not; and it shall be given unto him" (James 1:5).

One successful Christian educator tells an interesting story that explains the need for sympathetic understanding and genuine tact.

"John was full of mischief. He was happy when he was making faces or playing pranks. His Sunday school teacher could do little with him or with the class, for he kept it in a constant uproar with his amusing performances. 'Look at him now!' she complained to the superintendent. Sure enough, in the center of a group of grinning boys, his facial contortions and comical antics were a source of great enjoyment. 'That's the monkey,' said the superintendent, as he went down to see what he could do. He grabbed the boy by the collar and shook him vigorously, while he told the boy that the Sunday school was no place for monkeys, and that if he did not keep quiet and behave himself, he would have to be put out of the school.

"Immediately the boy became sullen, obstinate, silent. His teacher could not get him to speak a word throughout the rest of the hour. After Sunday school, when she reported his obstinacy to the superintendent, he said, 'That's the mule!' However, the superintendent decided to call at the boy's home and have a talk with the mother. He went the next morning when he thought the boy would be in school. Imagine his surprise when, in a dilapidated little house, he found this boy at the washtub helping his mother to work.

'I have come to see you about John,' He said.

'Oh!' said the mother, tears filling her eyes, 'I don't know what I would do without him. Since his father died, he has helped me with my washings, which are our only means of support. My health is so poor that were it not for him, I do not know what I would do.'

"The superintendent did not say what he had intended to say. Instead he remarked, 'There, that's the man.'"

The wise teacher will plan, work, teach, and pray that the grace of God will transform each pupil in his class. The problems, disciplines, and sacrifices will all be forgotten in the joy of watching his pupils accept Christ and "grow in grace."

"Take fast hold of instruction [discipline]; *let her not go; keep her; for she is thy life"* (Proverbs 4:13).

Suggested Questions for Review

1. How is discipline related to moral and spiritual development?
2. In what ways do disorderly pupils interfere with the work of the Lord?
3. What factors lead to disorder in a classroom?
4. How can a teacher help create an atmosphere of order?
5. Describe at least four types of disorderly pupils.
6. Discuss the thoughtless pupil, and how his need may be met.
7. How should the problem of the restless pupil be met?
8. What can be done about the needs of the self-centered pupil?
9. How can a teacher deal with a malicious pupil?

Additional Exploration

1. Bring a specific, current problem among pupils for class discussion and possible solution. Describe the actions, determine the causes, and seek for workable solutions. Discuss the teacher's personal responsibility for helping these problem pupils.
2. Discuss objectively some factors in your church that cause discomforts, distractions, and disturbances. Seek workable solutions. On things that can't be changed, seek for proper attitudes and acceptance of situations.

3. Evaluate objectively your own appearance, mannerisms, teaching. List any factors that might create disorder. Take steps to correct these.

CHAPTER ELEVEN

Applying the Truth

The educational process involves four major steps: acquisition, assimilation, appropriation, and application. The *acquisition* of knowledge is like the hasty reading of a book. It is *assimilated* by further reading and study until it is fully understood and remembered. By marking and filing certain passages for future use, there is an *appropriation* of knowledge. Finally, when its teachings are quoted or its truths are reproduced in life, there is the *application* of knowledge.

The real test of teaching is not what a pupil hears, but what he becomes. Education is not merely the acquisition of knowledge but its use. An educator "leads out" so that the pupil learns the facts and actually applies them to his own life.

The Christian teacher has the tremendous responsibility of helping to shape the lives of his pupils. To do this, he teaches the Word of God. His task is not completed when he has imparted Bible knowledge. He must go on to help his pupils develop Christian character and maturity. He looks for response in the *life* of each pupil. When godliness is manifested, the teacher knows that the Word of God has been effectual and that the lessons have been learned.

It is impossible to separate Christian character from Christian living. As character develops, it is expressed in living. The outward Christian life is the result of the Christ-formed character within. When Christ is acknowledged as Lord, the pupil will be mastered by God's truth and will establish the habits of study, prayer, reverence, worship, obedience, and unselfishness.

An urgent desire to cultivate these habits should motivate the Christian teacher.

Christian character grows by expression—not through dreaming or wishing or talking. The habit of doing nothing is as devastating as the habit of doing wrong. If instruction and inspiration are not expressed in action, they will destroy spiritual sensitivity and make it extremely difficult to respond to the Holy Spirit's leading. Expressional activities must infiltrate the teaching program, so that positive, active Christian character will be encouraged and developed.

Christ's teaching methods include a strong emphasis on application. In the Sermon on the Mount He said, "Whosoever heareth these saying of mine, and *doeth* them, I will liken him unto a wise man, which built his house upon a rock" (Matthew 7:24). "Not every one that saith unto me, Lord, Lord, shall enter into the kingdom of heaven; but he that *doeth* the will of my Father which is in heaven" (Matthew 7:21). "By their fruits ye shall know them" (Matthew 7:20). He taught his disciples that the inner spiritual condition is manifested by outward deeds and actions. They did not learn this truth in a formal schoolroom. They shared His life and work. They lived as He lived. They learned right attitudes toward God and their fellow men. They sensed His motives and ministry. Then He sent them out to complete their training by practical experience in everyday life.

In the same way, Sunday school pupils form Christian habits. They learn to pray, not by defining or describing prayer, but by entering actively into prayer. They learn how to study God's Word by actual use of the Bible. They become reverent, obedient, unselfish by *practicing* these virtues.

In making the application, there are three considerations.

APPLICATION OF THE WORD OF GOD The Word of God provides the principles and power for Christian living. It is useless to attempt to build Christian character independent of its instruction. In their zeal for "applied truth," some educators have lost sight of Biblical content. Their attention is focused on the pupils' experiences. They intimate that the Bible is not suited for modern application. But the Bible is changeless in every changing age. It is "profitable for doctrine, for reproof, for correction, for instruction in righteousness" (II Timothy 3:16). The human "heart is deceitful above all things and desperately wicked" (Jeremiah 17:9). Pupils cannot build Christian faith on the foundation of everyday human experiences. The Bible is the chart and compass.

The Bible deals with life by recognizing sin and supplying God's remedy. It touches every inner and outer area—sports, social activities, home, school, church. Modern educators, both Christian and secular, ought to realize that the Bible meets life's greatest needs. Bible-centered lessons aimed at life-centered needs provide the most effective curriculums.

Our Lord laid great stress on "application," based on the Word of God. When He went into the synagogue at Nazareth (Luke 4:16-21), He read and expounded the first two verses of Isaiah 61. His exposition provided an up-to-date application. He said that the words of this ancient prophet were fulfilled that *very day*. Years later, after His resurrection, when He met the disappointed disciples on the road to Emmaus, He drew out from them the reason for their perplexity. He met their real life situation and comforted the sorrowful disciples by "expounding unto them in all the Scriptures the things concerning Himself" (Luke 24:27). This was His method of Bible teaching. It was applied instruction. It was aimed at human need. David R. Piper has said:

"We must put equal emphasis on two facts which are not contradictory but correlative in Jesus' method. He taught Scripture directly by the expository method and used the Scripture as authority, and yet He taught for the specific purpose of applying the meaning of Scripture to some real life question, problem, or need of those whom He addressed."

APPLICATION TO THE TEACHER No teacher can successfully apply truth to his pupils until he has first applied it to his own life. Pupils must constantly see exemplified in their teacher the Biblical truths he seeks to apply to their lives. This is a categorical imperative in Christian teaching. Dr. J. McConaughey says:

"If our pupils are to learn of Christ through us, we must be sure that we really know Him ourselves—that we have been saved from sin by His death on the Cross, and are kept from falling into sin by the help which He daily gives us."

The Lord Jesus accompanied His teaching by a constant demonstration of the truth. He taught humility by the object lesson—placing a child in the midst of His quarreling, ambitious disciples. He exemplified meekness by girding Himself and washing the disciples' feet (John 13:15). He frequently taught forgiveness (Matthew 6:15; 18:21, 22), but it was in His look of forgiveness, after Peter had denied His Lord that the impetuous disciple learned its real meaning (Luke 22:61, 62).

Christ demonstrated forgiveness on the cross when He prayed, "Father, forgive them, for they know not what they do." And, even the hardened centurion acknowledged that Jesus was a righteous man (Luke 23:34, 47). Christ taught about prayer, but His disciples failed to understand until "it came to pass, that, *as he was praying* in a certain place, when he ceased, one of his disciples said unto him, Lord, teach us to pray, as John also taught his disciples" (Luke 11:1).

Many young people have testified that while they forgot the verbal instruction received in their youth, they could never forget the picture of a mother kneeling in intercessory prayer. The teacher's daily life must demonstrate his instruction in order to impress the hearts and minds of his pupils. Truths that have not helped the teacher will not help the class. The lesson must first affect the teacher before it can bless the class.

Teacher, examine yourself by asking, "What has this lesson taught me? Am I better qualified for my work because I have studied this lesson? Do I exemplify the truth I am teaching to my class?" Marion Lawrance says, "This is the crucial part of a teacher's preparation, for after all, the teacher's life is the life of his teaching."

Many an otherwise fine Christian worker or Sunday school teacher has nullified his ministry by some annoying idiosyncrasy or by a failure to apply God's Word to his life.

APPLICATION TO THE PUPIL The application of the lesson is vitally related to the teacher's aim. In lesson preparation, the teacher should plan to meet the specific needs of his pupils, both as a class and as individuals. In order to do this, the application of instruction must be aimed in several directions.

A. Salvation

It is imperative that every pupil understand his personal responsibility for a decision for Christ. All instruction should train him in the truths and procedures that will prepare for personal acceptance of Jesus Christ as Saviour and Lord.

B. Spirituality

After his conversion, the pupil should be given opportunities to "grow in grace." Regular attendance at Sunday school should result in systematic Bible study and prayer.

Regardless of organizational setup, the Sunday school should provide training in worship. Individuals or classes may plan and lead the assembly. This will involve a study of the elements of worship, a search of the Scripture for the acts involved in worship, and an observation of the worship program of the church. It will require an evaluation of the prayers, hymns, devotional books, and periodicals that will help all pupils to understand and appreciate the experiences of worship.

The entire Sunday school should also be encouraged to share the enjoyment of singing the hymns and Gospel songs of the church. Almost everyone can sing—all can respond to the appeal of music adapted to their understanding.

Instruction must be given in personal prayer life if pupils are to "grow in grace and in the knowledge of our Lord and Saviour, Jesus Christ" (II Peter 3:18). Pupils should participate in group praying during the class period. This will develop prayer habits and encourage them to be faithful in private devotions.

C. Stewardship

The development of spiritual life involves the pupil's personal responsibility for his use of time, abilities, and possessions. He should be taught to support the entire program of the church. He should learn to contribute his own money. The pupil's real sharing of *his* possessions creates the best impression. And—even if his parents provide his offerings, the pupil should be taught true stewardship.

Leaders and teachers need to learn that they are "raising" children and not money. Insomuch as the spirit of sacrificial sharing permeates the entire Sunday school, the pupils will learn and practice the full stewardship of time, talent, and things.

In Sunday school, we must train each generation to be liberal, systematic, cheerful givers. The pupils need information about the object of their gifts as well as the "why" of their giving, so that they will practice Christian stewardship.

> "Not what we give, but what we share,
> For the gift without the giver is bare;
> He who gives himself with his gifts feeds three,
> Himself, his hungering neighbor, and Me."

D. Service

An adequate curriculum, properly taught, should lead the pupil to a personal responsibility for his talents. The wise teacher knows how to capture every opportunity to find something worthwhile for his pupils to do. He makes his instruction a laboratory course in Christian service as a stimulus for lifetime surrender to Christ.

1. Home

Christians need to live for Christ in their own homes. Children should realize their responsibility for its happiness. They should be encouraged to participate in the care of the home, and warned against shirking their duty. The entire family should share in the hospitality which the home extends to friends and neighbors, and take pride in demonstrating its attractiveness.

2. Church

Each pupil should be impressed with his responsibility to the church, especially if he is a member. This implies regular attendance; systematic proportionate contributions to its support; and active participation in its program. Pupils should be encouraged to secure new members for the Sunday school and visit those who attend irregularly or have dropped out entirely.

In a wide-awake Sunday school, there are many other duties for members of all ages. Service can be rendered in the distribution of supplies or the decoration of the rooms for special occasions. Older pupils can help to build up enrollment with a community survey or census.

3. Community

There are many service opportunities in every community. The Sunday school should minister to the needy, the sick, the lonely. It should promote a well-rounded program to meet the total needs of children, young people, and adults. It should have a part in civic and community enterprises. These provide valuable opportunities for the Sunday school's "practical work."

4. World

The church and Sunday school should extend the Gospel into the whole world. There are many things to be done for people in other lands. Letters, missionary boxes, and gifts of money can express genuine and intelligent interest in the lives of others. Pupils must be brought to see their responsibility for evangelizing the entire world. They should be urged to obey Christ's commission, "Go ye therefore, and teach all nations . . . Teaching them to observe all things whatsoever I have commanded you . . ." (Matthew 28:19, 20).

CHRISTIAN EDUCATION

The *heart* of Christian education
   Is the education of the heart,
Teaching true regeneration.
   This is where all men must start,
If they would reach the consummation
   And be like Him, every part.

The *soul* of Christian education
   Is the training of the soul
Reaching life's full expectation
   In such cleansing of the whole
That all living's a vocation
   With Christlikeness as the goal.

The *aim* of Christian education
   Is the changing of life's aim,
Till the day of graduation
   From this world—its sin—its shame.
What a wondrous destination
   To be saved in Jesus' Name.

So give them Christian education.
   This the education that men need
To deliver from frustration
   As Christ's blood they daily plead.
Then—in peaceful occupation
   They will learn to LIVE indeed.
               —D. K. Reisinger

Suggested Questions for Review

1. List and define four steps in the educational process.
2. What did Christ say about the relationship of knowledge and actions?
3. How can the Christian teacher help his pupils form Christian habits?
4. Why must lesson applications be based on the Word of God?
5. Illustrate how Christ accompanied his teaching by demonstration of truth.

6. Why must the Sunday school teacher first apply Bible truth to his own life?
7. List four general needs of pupils that the teacher should plan to meet in lesson application.
8. How can pupils be guided to understand and experience worship?
9. In what ways can stewardship be taught?
10. Where may pupils find service opportunities to practice the truths they are taught?

Additional Exploration

1. Trace Jesus' teaching in the Gospels and list at least five instances where His teaching was put into immediate practice. For instance, Blind Bartimaeus' immediate response to Jesus' command (Mark 10:46-52). List three instances where His teaching was applied later. For instance, Christ's charge to Peter to "feed my sheep" (John 21:15-17).
2. Examine several Sunday school lesson quarterlies for various departments to see how the authors apply lesson truths to life situations. With each quarterly list at least one additional possible application.
3. Using illustrations secured from teachers in your own church or your own experience, justify the statement, "The real test of teaching is what a pupil becomes."

CHAPTER TWELVE

Testing the Teaching

Modern education minimizes the value of drill unless it is meaningful and functional. Everyone recognizes the importance of practice in order to become skillful in playing the piano, or playing baseball, or driving a car. Testing still holds a prominent place in today's schools. In fact, there is little teaching without testing.

Most Sunday school teachers, however, would be shocked to discover by any simple testing procedure, how little knowledge is actually retained by their pupils. They may be entirely oblivious to the fact that much of their instruction is ineffective. Public school educators are keenly aware of this great deficiency in the Sunday school. Christian educators are also becoming alarmed.

Sometime ago a questionnaire on Bible facts was given to 850 high school students. Sixty-four percent did not know that Moses was the world's greatest lawgiver. Eighty-three percent did not know why Gethsemane is important in Bible history. Seventy-eight percent could not quote two verses from the Bible. Fifty-eight percent could not name five books of the Bible. Forty-eight percent could not name one writer of the Bible.

Dr. Dobbins gave a similar test to 81 sophomores and juniors in high school—all of whom were regular Sunday school attendants. The average grade was 35%. The questions were purely factual. Who was the first man? Name the Pentateuch. Who led the children of Israel from Egypt? Who was the first king of Israel? Who wrote most of the Psalms? Name the four Gospels. Name four of Paul's epistles.[1]

In another public school, an eighth-grade social studies class was studying the battle of Waterloo. One pupil, in his enthusiasm, spoke of the "Calvary" charge. Immediately the teacher wrote two words on the chalkboard—cavalry and Calvary. She asked the meaning of the first word. Every pupil knew the correct answer. "Now," she said, "here is the word that John used. Tell me what it means to you." There was no reply. Finally one boy raised his hand and mentioned the name of a local cemetery. Another thought it was a city in Canada (Calgary).

The teacher was plainly disappointed. "How many of you boys and girls go to Sunday school?" she asked. Practically every hand was raised. "And

---

[1]Gaines S. Dobbins, *The Improvement of Teaching in the Sunday School* (Nashville: Broadman Press, 1955), p. 153.

do you mean to tell me that you never heard of Calvary? It seems that you would know the importance of that place in the Bible just as you know the importance of Waterloo in history, or of New York in geography."

"If teaching is careless, superficial, blundering, the results will be reflected in the failure of our pupils to grasp the truths they should learn, and in the consequent impoverishment of their lives. If our teaching is earnest, thoughtful, skillful, the results will be manifest in the growth and development of our pupils as they incorporate the truths of Christianity in their character and conduct."[2]

Sooner or later every teacher's effectiveness will be judged, not only of men, but also of God. Those who teach cannot escape the testing of their work and workmanship. (Read I Corinthians 3:1-15.)

Testing a pupil's knowledge is quite as possible as teaching him the truth. Those who actually test their teaching will find that the major difficulty is the inadequacy of their own preparation. In planning a testing program, it is of primary importance that the teacher impress the pupil with the things he wishes him to remember. Much of the testing may be done by means of a well-conducted recitation.

THE RECITATION This is one effective teaching method. It is also a good method for testing the pupil's knowledge. By testing this knowledge, we "put it on trial." We submit the pupil's understanding to cross-examination to determine whether it is clear or confused. Recitation should not be a mere repetition of exact words or phrases. Pupils should be encouraged to say in their own way what they understand to be the truth. The test should be thorough, searching, correct, and inspiring if the teacher is to obtain a true picture of the pupil's understanding.

The teacher must be alert to attitudes and knowledge as expressed by these responses. Often a pupil's misunderstanding of one word or phrase will break the connection, and the teacher cannot proceed with further teaching until it has been explained.

Two areas must be considered when the recitation is used for testing.

A. Preparation for recitation

In public school, the previously-assigned lesson is the basis for the class session. "But," you ask, "how can we get *Sunday school pupils* to study at home?" Dr. Edge replies, "Just expect it. Often we get not because we expect not."[3]

If recitation is to be effective, at least five minutes should be spent in making assignments. Unless this is done, there cannot be a willing, intelligent response from the class. Pupils need guidance, assistance, and a clear, concise assignment, especially if they are expected to study at home.

[2]*Ibid.*, p. 150.
[3]Edge, *Teaching for Results*, p. 35.

B. Conducting the recitation

Who shall be called upon to recite, and in what order? A wise teacher does not indicate in advance which pupil is to be called on. He may call on the same pupil twice in succession in order to keep the class on the alert. Such uncertainty requires each pupil to follow closely the response of all others. The assignment is never made until the question has been asked or the topic stated. No pupil is overlooked nor called on too frequently.

Never use the "concert" or the "consecutive" methods. In the former, a few prepared pupils will lead the answers and the others will join in. In the latter, the only pupils who give close attention are those who are reciting or expecting to be called upon next.

Taking for granted that there has been home preparation and previous study, how will the teacher conduct the recitation? There are two methods which may be employed.

1. Question method

By the wise use of the question, the teacher will unfold the subject systematically and logically. Questions should not be stereotype. They will, to a large extent, be prompted by the response of the pupil. This will provide freshness and spontaneity.

2. Topical method

The topical method is a good test of expression. It compels the pupil to state his opinions, but makes him responsible for organizing his own thoughts and expressing them. Skillful teacher guidance will keep the class from being "sidetracked" into unrelated discussions. Combining the question and the topical methods will test what the pupil knows and provide him with an opportunity to defend his opinion.

THE EXAMINATION Public schools, colleges, and universities give final examinations. The work of a term, a semester, or even a year, is subject to a general review and examination. This is a commonly accepted practice and needs no defense among educators or leaders in business and professional circles.

Bible knowledge should be obtained and tested by the same methods used in other teaching areas. Many Sunday schools, however, are still reluctant to test the attainments of their pupils.

The Bible teaches that children should be brought up "in the nurture and *admonition* of the Lord" (Ephesians 6:4). Nurture involves knowledge. Admonition refers to behavior. There should be examinations in both of these fields.

The word *examination* creates terror in many people. They remember the wearisome, last-minute cramming. They recall the painful experience of trying to put on paper what had been laboriously and hurriedly memorized. They can't forget the questions they never anticipated and the problems they left blank. Little wonder that Sunday school teachers and pupils

TESTING THE TEACHING 89

alike have avoided these wearisome ordeals. Yet, if we take Sunday school work seriously, if our teaching is earnest, thoughtful, and skillful, we should use every objective method of testing. This includes the examination.

> "Only a well-designed examination comes close to requiring a student to function as an educated man . . . Only a comprehensive essay examination makes any pretense of testing wholes, or of presenting problems as they actually occur in the real life of the mind."[4]

And, in addition, teachers may require the preparation of a term paper, with a bibliography to show research work. This independent study has genuine educational value.

BIBLE TESTS The teacher prepares the questions and judges the answers. He may assign topics and evaluate the response. Pupils are accustomed to written tests in public school. Why not use them in the Sunday school? Some people argue that Sunday school is on a voluntary basis, that pupils may resent examinations, or that tests must be burdensome and obnoxious. The teacher who understands modern testing procedures knows that they are interesting, fascinating, stimulating, revealing, and extremely profitable.

A. Fields

Pupils should be tested in at least three areas of Bible knowledge.

1. Historical

There are many historical facts in the Bible narrative. These should be studied chronologically. For examination purposes, the facts may be "jumbled" and the student asked to rearrange them in logical order until they are impressed upon his mind.

2. Biographical

The pupils may be asked to identify Bible characters, arrange the names in chronological order, or supply missing information or events.

3. Geographical

Provide an outline map so that pupils can locate the cities, sections, and countries where important Biblical events took place. Small maps may be mimeographed, purchased, or drawn by the students. It is important that all pupils be familiar with the geographical factors connected with their Bible study.

B. Types of tests

Many types of standardized tests have been used successfully in public education and in other secular fields. These methods have been adapted for use in Sunday school. Usually the publishers of Sunday school literature

---

[4]Bestor, *The Restoration of Learning*, p. 336.

include suggested tests in pupils' or teachers' manuals. There are at least four types of tests which pupils undertake spontaneously.

1. True—False

In this type of test the student reads a series of statements. Some are true, some false. The student evaluates and circles the correct answer. The following suggested test is based on Luke 2:47-52:

The wise doctors in the temple were surprised at the wisdom shown in Jesus' answers.	T	F
He asked Mary and Joseph, "How is it that ye sought me?"	T	F
Jesus said He had to be about His Father's business.	T	F
Mary and Joseph did not understand what He told them.	T	F
The doctors said, "Stay with us."	T	F
Jesus stayed in Jerusalem at the Temple after Mary and Joseph found Him.	T	F
Jesus went home with His parents to Nazareth.	T	F
Jesus was obedient to (subject unto) His parents.	T	F
His mother forgot all about what had happened.	T	F
Jesus kept growing in wisdom and stature, and in favor with God and man.	T	F

2. Completion

Completion tests are more exacting than true-false tests. In the true-false test there is a 50% chance of guessing right. In completion tests, the pupil fills in the information indicated by blank spaces. The following example is suggestive of what might be done after studying II Kings 20.

Hezekiah was sick unto ....

The prophet who came to see Hezekiah was ....

The prophet told Hezekiah that he was going to ....

Hezekiah sadly turned his face to ....

Hezekiah prayed that God would remember he had walked in ....

As Hezekiah prayed, he ....

3. Multiple choice

Multiple choice tests offer a fine opportunity to discover the pupil's knowledge. Here is a sample geographical test. The pupil underscores the name of the correct answer.

Village that didn't see many mighty works because of unbelief?
   Jerusalem, Nazareth, Capernaum, Bethsaida.
Mountain on which Jesus gave the Beatitudes?
   Kurn, Hattin, Mt. Olympus, Mt. Hermon, Mt. Zion.

TESTING THE TEACHING 91

    Province through which the Jews hated to pass?
      Berea, Judea, Galilee, Samaria.
    Village where Jesus was always welcome?
      Bethany, Nazareth, Gergesa, Jericho.
    Body of water that obeyed Jesus' command?
      The Great Sea, Dead Sea, Sea of Galilee, Jordan River.
    Region that had a revival because a man told what Jesus did for him?
      Syria, Decapolis, Caesarea Philippi, Wilderness.

4. Matching

The matching test is usually popular with the pupils. It requires nothing more than the use of lines or numbers. In the following example, the pupil is told that the book of Philemon contains the names and identifying statements of eleven persons. He is asked to match these by drawing a line from the name to the correct statement.

    1. The "brother" whose greeting Paul sent   Paul
    2. Runaway slave   Timothy
    3. Philemon's wife   Philemon
    4. Philemon's son   Onesimus
    5. A great missionary in prison   Apphia
    6. A rich man of Colosse   Archippus
    7. A fellow-prisoner of Paul   Epaphras
    8. Paul's fellow-laborers   Mark, Aristarchus
                                                                     Demas, Luke

BEHAVIOR TESTS The tests just studied are used basically to determine the pupil's knowledge of Bible content. In Sunday school work, we should also desire to measure spiritual growth and behavior. This is more difficult because life consists largely of habits of thinking, feeling, or acting that have become deeply rooted through repetition. Children need assistance in the formation of right habits. Sunday school teachers need the co-operation of the parents in this important responsibility. Jesus emphasized this phase of Christian instruction when He said, "Whosoever heareth these sayings of mine, *and doeth them,* I will liken him unto a wise man, which built his house upon a rock" (Matthew 7:24).

A. Sunday school records

Successful Sunday schools are never satisfied with mere records of attendance. Several excellent systems have been developed to record additional information, including the interest and response of pupils. These systems tabulate such items as lesson preparation, church attendance, family background, punctuality, use of Bible, prayer life, soul winning, enlisting new pupils, and offering.

These records may not measure results in the life of the pupil, but they do indicate some areas that contribute to Christian character.

B. Character building

After a pupil has accepted the Lord Jesus Christ, it is essential that he be shown how to relate his faith and his works. "Even so faith, if it hath not works, is dead, being alone" (James 2:17).

"The supreme achievement of Christian education is well-rounded Christian character. By Christian character we mean that habits, knowledge, attitudes, choices, and conduct are organized around Christ as the center, so that all life is under His control. The attainment of this ideal is not instantaneous but progressive. Progress toward it is to be measured by character tests.

"Self-rating scales are popular and useful in helping one discover one's strong and weak points. Just as one looks in a mirror to check upon personal appearance, so one might profitably use a series of questions to determine inner qualities of character."[5]

Pupils should be encouraged to check their own Christian lives. They should be taught to be strictly honest and objective. A check mark beside certain "virtues and vices" will represent each day's actions. They should be taught to grade themselves realistically.

	S.	M.	T.	W.	TH.	F.	S.		S.	M.	T.	W.	TH.	F.	S.
Pride								Humility							
Narrowness								"Bigness"							
Intolerance								Tolerance							
Selfishness								Unselfishness							
Anger								Self-control							
Revenge								Love							
Thoughtlessness								Thoughtfulness							
Impoliteness								Courtesy							
Worrying								Peace							
Grumbling								Joy							
Cheating								Honesty							

ATTITUDE AND CHOICE Sunday school teaching should lead to the formation of Christian attitudes and choices. It is necessary to test these outcomes, but it is not easy to measure progress in these spiritual realms. Regeneration and "growth in grace" are produced by the Holy Spirit. Who can fathom His mysterious operations or know the

---

[5]Dobbins, *ibid.*, pp. 161, 162.

time when conviction is brought to the heart? The teacher must be sensitive to the moods of the class. He must know how to take advantage of that psychological moment when the Holy Spirit reveals that the moment of decision has come. Under God, the consecrated, discerning teacher will have the joy of leading his pupils to the saving knowledge of the Lord Jesus Christ. He may also lead them to the place where their lives are surrendered to the perfect will of God. This is the ultimate aim and outcome of Bible-centered, Christ-honoring teaching.

Suggested Questions for Review

1. Why is testing an important part of Bible teaching?
2. How can class recitation be utilized for testing purposes?
3. What is the possible place of the essay in Bible testing?
4. In what areas of Bible knowledge should the pupil be tested?
5. Describe the merits of each of four types of Bible tests.
6. Describe how Sunday school records are in reality behaviour tests.
7. Define and illustrate a character-building check chart.

Additional Exploration

1. Write your reaction to one of the following life situations for possible future class discussion.
    A fifth-grader tempted to cheat in a school examination.
    A teen-ager unwilling to assume his share of home responsibility.
    A young person driving a car without parents' permission or without a driver's license.
   Report group decisions to entire class for further consideration of character principles.
2. Prepare a list of problematic life situations at various age levels, the response to which would indicate the measure of a student's spiritual development.
3. Investigate Christian education testing programs for helpful data concerning methods of testing. It may be necessary to contact several denominational and interdenominational groups.
4. Discuss helpful ways to enlist the cooperation of pupils in a program of testing in Biblical truths.

FOR YOUR INFORMATION

Evangelical Teacher Training Association was organized in 1930 to strengthen and advance evangelical Christian education. From the beginning, E.T.T.A. has pioneered in Bible-centered, Christ-honoring leadership preparation materials to preserve and propagate the rich Gospel *message* through the best educational *methods*.

Christian education is presented as an important factor in the fulfillment of Christ's commission "Go ye therefore, and *teach* all nations . . . *teaching* them to observe all things, whatsoever I have commanded you" (Matt. 28:19, 20). In order to minister to the greatest number in the advancement of Christian education, E.T.T.A. functions on three educational levels, each of which complements the others.

THE PRELIMINARY CERTIFICATE COURSE Designed for local church and community leadership preparation classes, summer Christian education conferences and camps, this course is the road to successful teaching for Sunday school teachers and officers. Six vital and challenging subjects are covered—three on Bible Survey and three on Christian Education.

Bible Survey These practical Bible Survey studies are foundational. They show the marvelous unity of the 66 books of the Bible and help one grasp the central teaching that binds books, chapters, and verses together.

    OLD TESTAMENT SURVEY—Law and History
    OLD TESTAMENT SURVEY—Poetry and Prophecy
    NEW TESTAMENT SURVEY

Christian Education These subjects give insight into the pupil's personality, problems, ambitions, and needs; give the "know-how" of teaching; present the overall purpose, organization, and program of the Sunday school.

>UNDERSTANDING CHILDREN AND YOUTH
>TEACHING TECHNIQUES
>SUNDAY SCHOOL SUCCESS

A Credit Card is awarded upon completion of each unit that is taught by an approved E.T.T.A. teacher. The Preliminary Teachers Certificate is granted when the required 6 units have been completed.

To assure credit for work satisfactorily completed, teachers of courses must be approved in advance by the Association. All holders of E.T.T.A. Diplomas granted by member schools* are already approved. Most pastors and Christian education directors because of their training and experience are approved upon application. Others with qualifying training and experience may be approved upon recommendation of their pastor. Send for free packet of information telling how to start E.T.T.A. classes.

THE ADVANCED CERTIFICATE COURSE Following the Preliminary Certificate Course, the Advanced Certificate Course gives a deeper understanding of God's Word and an insight into fields of Christian service. It is offered in E.T.T.A. affiliated Bible institutes* and is also profitably presented in local church or community classes. The Course consists of a minimum of 12 units, each 12 chapters in length and leads to the Advanced Teachers Certificate. It includes the 6 units of the Preliminary Certificate Course and the following 6 units.

>THE MISSIONARY ENTERPRISE
>SUNDAY SCHOOL EVANGELISM
>THE TRIUNE GOD (Doctrine Vol. 1)
>BIBLICAL BELIEFS (Doctrine Vol. 2)
>VACATION BIBLE SCHOOL
>YOUR BIBLE (Bible Introduction)

THE STANDARD TRAINING COURSE These 24 semester hours in the study of Christian education include basic and extensive Bible courses as well as a wide selection of courses in the principles, history, and methods of Christian education and related subjects. This Course is offered only in institutions of higher education which hold Active membership in E.T.T.A.* A Teachers Diploma is awarded in recognition of required educational attainment and qualifies the holder to conduct the E.T.T.A. leadership preparation program in church or community classes.

---

* *A list of all Member Schools is available on request.*

NOTES